WHY MY MOTHER WENT AWAY

Why My Mother Went Away

A Memoir

Alan Kennedy

Lasserrade Press

www.lasserradepress.com

Paperback ISBN 978-1-9996941-7-3
ePub ISBN 978-1-9996941-9-0

First published in the United Kingdom by Lasserrade Press 2025

Contents

For Elizabeth

I experience a feeling of happiness such as it is quite impossible to imagine in a normal state and which other people have no idea of ... and this feeling is so strong and so delightful that for a few seconds of such bliss one would gladly give up ten years of one's life, if not one's whole life.

Dostoevsky, *The Idiot.*

And I knew such a man, (whether in the body, or out of the body, I cannot tell: God knoweth;) how that he was caught up into paradise, and heard unspeakable words, which it is not lawful for a man to utter.

Saint Paul, *Letter to the Corinthians* 12:1-4

Ecstasy is a dysfunction in error prediction, resulting in a feeling of peace, well-being, and clarity, due to impaired integration of multisensory and interoceptive stimuli.

Arias M. *Neurología.* 2019; 34: 55-61.

But the only truth clear to me in that dark time, the only truth which I had to accept, was that incisions had been made through the prefrontal lobes of my brain, that area which is the seat of human foresight, creativity and responsibility; that the damage done might have permanently impaired the faculties which made me particularly human and, above all, particularly me; that I had no way of ever knowing what I might have been without those incisions; that what I was now, after those incisions, was all I had to start with.

Ronald Senator, *Requiem Letters.*

Chapter 1

I am in my pram, sitting too high up, with Mother behind me steering us over the bumpy ground leading to the Nursery School. It is awkward because I am crammed in with Ian. He is lying wedged at the front wearing a blue hat to keep the sun off his eyes. That is my hat. A hat so much a part of me that when Mother snatched it off it was as if he had been given my head. Her concern for this tiresome baby is inexplicable and I am vexed. He cries continually and can only be comforted by being taken in her arms and walked up and down. Which is to ignore me. Placed in my room at night, another violent intrusion, he refuses to sleep and fills the house with plaintive little wails until Father comes and takes the baby and his basket into their bedroom. And I must then fall asleep on my own, listening to indistinct bickering, Father talking endlessly, Mother managing a word or two, the little wail accompanying the two of them.

Every day now Ian is in the pram for the trip to Mother's school. Sometimes, only Ian in the pram and me jerked along in my harness, my legs not quite always on the ground. Mother rocks the pram as she goes to soothe the passenger, who now wails outdoors. When we arrive, I go in with Mother. Ian is left in the pram and we hear his faint wailing most of the morning. Mother puts me at the back of the class, sitting on the lino floor. If she remembers, I get the string of cowrie shells to play with; mostly, she forgets.

She has stopped laughing. She doesn't laugh at all now. If she seems angry I know she is not pretending, which was more fun. She no longer lets me win the race to the wooden gate because we don't race any more. She sits by the fire, joggling the wail on her knee and even cries a little herself. Which at first seems sensible, then I begin to feel mothers should not cry and it starts to be frightening.

The fireplace in the living room in Leabrook Road has little metal ovens at its sides, each with its own door, and places for pots and pans on top. Not that Mother would dream of cooking there. Poor people cooked in the living room. We live in ours and Mother cooks in the draughty and inconvenient kitchen. She has started to break the rule. Most afternoons she has laid a fire in the little stove to heat a saucepan on one of the metal rings, filling the house with a sharp unpleasant medicinal smell. I don't know why this is being done. I don't know why she is drinking this stuff. I ask her and she says it's a tonic for her nerves. Bought at Wednesbury market. But I don't know what a tonic is. I think she is drinking whatever is in the pan to hold at bay something stalking her, closing in on her, stifling her.

The wail no longer even starts the night with me. He has his permanent station in their bedroom. Father insists he has his own little bed, but he wets his sheets and cries to come out. Most mornings white bundles are left in a pile by the kitchen door for Mother to wash in the copper in the shed. She pegs them out in the sooty air. Each day she drinks her brew. She has started to sleep in her chair at the wrong time of day. Once she is even late to school, the pram bouncing so much on the path that his howls bring the other teachers to the window to watch us as we scuttle across the playground, me alongside, hanging on, my legs aching with the walk.

I have been asleep. There was talk of a raid. I don't know this word with its raspy sound, but it frightens me because Mother runs out of the room shouting something I could not understand. She has Ian in her arms. Everything is a muddle because it is Father's night to wear a strange square canvas box, the colour of clay, slung over his shoulder. And his metal hat. Before he goes he tells Stuart to put me to bed. He has never said that before and I go myself, not needing to be put anywhere. When I remember to come back to say good night god bless to Mother she is in the kitchen. She tells me to go to bed.

I have been asleep I don't know how long. There is an awful smell everywhere. The smell when the gas is on and no-one has lit it. I can hear Father shouting. Not inside the house, but outside. He seems to be in the street, not angry, but shouting. I can hear glass breaking and then voices, first Father then Stuart, then Mr Harrison. Why is Stuart allowed to be awake when it's dark? And I don't know at all why Mr

Harrison is in our house. And a woman's voice. Not Mother's. Not anyone I know. I hear Father on the first set of stairs and I sit up. He comes along the little corridor and runs upstairs again. He still has his big shoes on, that he always takes off and leaves in the kitchen. As my door opens, I suddenly know he wants to find me asleep. I don't know why I know this, but I am sure of it. I slide under the blanket and am asleep. I sense him standing over me. He is out of breath and muttering an endless incomprehensible monologue to himself. The light from the stairs streams onto my bed. He bends over me and comes very close. I give a little sigh and turn over and he stands up, mutters, and walks away. I hear him trying to open the window. He has forgotten that that window has never opened. Eventually he stops and comes to my bedside again. Then, creeping in an odd, slow, exaggerated way, he goes out and I hear him going down the stairs which creak under the weight of his boots.

In the morning the smell of gas has not quite gone. Stuart is having his breakfast. I have seen him look like that before. He knows something that I don't know and I know he will never tell me. Father is in the kitchen giving Ian his breakfast. It is strangely quiet. I am to know Mother is poorly and in bed. Stuart leaves to go to school and I am put outside to play. There are shards of broken glass in a cardboard box at the kitchen door. You can smell the linseed oil from putty where one of the panes in the kitchen door has been replaced.

The week Mother was in bed nothing was quite as it should be. Father went reluctantly to work, packing his canvas satchel with marmalade sandwiches himself. Breakfast was made by Aunt Lizzie, who put too much milk in everything. More shocking, she poured it from the bottle. I am allowed to cross the road on my own and walk to school feeling sick from milk, feeling sick that the world has become unhinged.

Mother has changed. She has no time to talk to me. She talks to Father with the kitchen door closed. Or to Stuart on his own. Vicar Bell comes to the house, without his black gown, knocking the front door, although no-one ever comes in that way because the door catches the carpet. Close to, he smells of church candles and cigarettes. Father takes him to the living room, leaving Ian and me to sit alone in the chilly front room, silent and tense, not talking, not reading, doing nothing. Father has wound the clock for the vicar's visit and we sit listening to the tick until he goes away. The house is horribly quiet.

*

My parents, Bob and Dot, had married in 1935, celebrated with a rain-soaked honeymoon on the Isle of Man. It had been the kind of Saxon-Celt match E.M. Forster thought ill-advised. Father's father had been a West coast Scot - Clan Cameron country - who had moved to the Midlands of England to open a pub, an event celebrated by providing Father with a sister, Winifred, some twenty years his junior. Father always claimed he was the seventh son of a seventh son (possibly he stretched this Biblical fiction even further, I forget) and had an almost mystical reverence for his Scottish ancestors. Mother was a Cowley, a name in the Domesday Book. I never met her father, who had died when she was child, but I remember my grandmother, who lived alone in Henley-in-Arden in a timber-framed house that had changed little since Shakespeare's time. The fact that there was no electricity and that water had to be hauled from a well in a bucket made visits extraordinarily exciting. We would come to blows over the right to sit on the shiny wooden seat perched terrifyingly over a deep hole smelling vaguely of disinfectant at the far end of the garden.

Given Father's pedigree, it seemed a foregone conclusion that the issue from my parents' union would be boys, albeit they drew the line long before seven. Mother, coming from a family of four girls, was confident that this time things would be different. She was wrong. As a kind of cosmic rejoinder Stuart Charles was born under her own sign of Pisces, on 25th February 1936. Father's favourite son, long before alternatives were even on offer. I was the first of these, coming into the world on the first of October 1939, as a cataclysmic war broke out. I was christened Robert Alan, a name which, while Scottish enough, Mother rejected. Rejected, that is, while pregnant, in the extremely unlikely event I would turn out to be a boy. My father's name was Robert and we would certainly have fallen to an Ocker Hill tradition and become the *Big Bob* and *Little Bob* of

Leabrook Road. To spare me this hypothetical indignity she had settled on *Nicholas John*, surely unaware that passing my school days as "knickerless" would be even worse.

I have no memory of the event, but apparently my baptism was a *coup de theatre*. An Anglican baptism in 1940 was a long-winded affair, the climax at the font coming only after a lengthy inquisition of all those present. My Godfather was our landlord's son. Perhaps it was his new Army uniform that intimidated my mother – we will never know - but when the vicar's solemn injunction *Name this child* boomed out, it precipitated only silence and nervous glances. Finally, my Father spoke the words: *Robert Alan*. By then the startled vicar had already unpinned the slip of paper attached to his sleeve, he may even have cast an anguished look at Mother, but it was too late: the deed was done. My infant sins, surely not all that many, were washed away with a Christian name I would never use.

I never discovered whether she forgave him. Perhaps it was not necessary, because my arrival itself gave her ample grounds for revenge. Disappointed by yet another unwanted boy, I became a kind of Betsey Trotwood. By the time Ian McColl brandished his Caledonian credentials on September 14th 1941, she had already determined to fashion as girlish a childhood for me as she could. Father was left to lump it, although he never did.

Home for we three boys in those war-time years, and for many years after, was a ramshackle rented house at 160, Leabrook Road in Ocker Hill, the end terrace of a row of four rather grim three-storey brick houses. They had been built by our benevolent landlord, a chain-smoking retired builder, Mr Harrison. He had formed the double terraced facade at one end into his own rather grand residence. The house in the middle was occupied by his daughter's family, which included two children (Roger and Elizabeth) of about our own age. Our house was a rambling, draughty, disorganised affair, with two living rooms a kitchen and bathroom on the ground floor, and (eventually) four bedrooms distributed over various levels above. Mr Harrison had built somewhat in the style of gothic novels, making use of whatever materials came his way, creating awkward passages, suicidally dangerous stairs, rickety shelves in unexpected places, and innumerable imposing panelled doors (acquired as a job lot) which led only to tiny cupboards.

These were, of course, days long before memories came in colour. Life in Leabrook Road was distinctly black-and-white. The place was irredeemably cold. When Father finally made a bedroom for me in a tiny attic on the third floor, the room was so chill in winter I recall melting fern patterns of ice before I could see through the windowpanes. Mother knew that I took the curtains down to reinforce my bed clothes because she helped me restore their wire supports in the morning, but that was as far as help would go. We were poor, but there were those poorer still. I had my share of blankets and there were no more.

The underpinnings of all four houses formed a cavernous cellar stretching the whole length of the building. There may once have been dividing walls but with the coming of war all but the floor supports had been knocked out, converting the space to a kind of psychological bomb shelter (it offered no physical shelter – a bomb would have buried the lot of us). So far as I know, war brought no German bombs to Ocker Hill; its greatest loss, in fact, had been self-inflicted, a misfired anti-aircraft shell falling through the chimney of a house, with many casualties. But we were not to know. Remember that, children of another age who now look back: *we were not to know.* Not knowing why, many a night - Ian swaddled, me in my portable cot – Stuart helped Mother scramble through the war-time clutter of a shelter that was nothing of the kind, in search of Mr Harrison's camp beds.

I will never know whether Father had a choice in the matter – probably not – but his decision to spend those wartime years fitfully sleeping on folded rugs in a damp cellar under a house in Leabrook Road was not entirely without consequence. Ours was a generation of children insidiously shaped by war: an abrupt change in diet left Stuart with a chronic skin condition and poor teeth. I was born allergic to milk leaving me susceptible to a multitude of infections. Ian's response to the ever-diminishing ration of food that came our way was a stubborn refusal to grow at all.

A major part of our section of the cellar was taken up by coal bins fashioned from railway sleepers, the coal arriving in clouds of black fog through a trap under the kitchen window. The rest of our allotted space served as Father's workshop and a place to store bottled food and the tinned things in food parcels sent by two of Mother's sisters who had fled to Canada. There were also pickled eggs kept in lines of scary white enamel buckets filled with viscous isinglass. Mother kept from us precisely what use she put them to. The eggs were our own, product of the little flock kept at the bottom of the garden and ruled over by a ferocious cockerel named Veronica, following a not uncommon medical uncertainty.

*

Ocker Hill is gone now, barely even a name on vintage maps, but for those who loved the place – and perhaps only those – it retains its status as a hamlet with romantic roots sunk deep into a vanished England. The place names of my childhood – Lea Brook, Doe Bank, Toll End, Bug Hole, Balls Hill, Summerhill, Riders Green, Pudding Green, Capponfield, Wednesbury Oak, Moat Farm – reached back even beyond a Saxon history: a place far more ancient than the steam engines, ironworks, coal pits and furnaces defining the Black Country. For my seven-year-old self stretched out on a quiet summer's day under the trees of Cannock Chase it seemed the green above my head went on for ever. Centuries earlier Ocker Hill was a clearing in a landscape made of trees. A thousand years ago the river Tame had petered out near Ocker Hill, trickling into much the same brooks as today; the walk from Wadensberie would take you past Lea Brook and Wall Brook and bifurcate at Cockle Brook. A few miles more would bring you to Secg's Leigh, or clearing. Sedgley now, where Mother and Father, before this story is done, will end their days.

Come out of the kitchen door of our house, walk down the narrow Dickensian passageway that divides 160, Leabrook Road from the cluster of more modest houses to its right, and I will show you Ocker Hill in 1946, the war done at last. Our house - three storeys of red brick - rears up on your left, daubed rather inexpertly in jet black pitch to keep the damp away. It is a passageway so narrow you can touch both sides with your seven-year-old outstretched arms. Open the wooden gate at the bottom - the gate a tiny boy once raced his

Mother to reach. It will be gone soon to allow bikes free passage, but not just yet, Stuart's first bike has only just arrived.

Step out onto the pavement and look down to your right, the road falling away in a gentle slope. You would be safe enough in the middle of the road - cars in Ocker Hill were still enough of a rarity to bring Mother to the window to look. The bus stop that would later take us to the Grammar School every day is not there yet. Heaps of horse manure are dotted down the road, marking the passage of brewers' drays. The pub just opposite our house is stocked up every day except Sunday. Walk that way down the gentle incline, passing little red brick houses, mysterious passageways and a sprinkling of tiny shops. First, a sweet shop at the top of a set of steps. There are no sweets to sell, but they sell newspapers and lamp oil and manage to stay open. A cobbler's shop further down is kept by Mr Bannister, the organist at St. Mark's church, a crabby bent man with a club foot corrected with a strange stepped boot of his own invention. At the bottom of the hill is a chemists shop, kept by a rakish man, usually a little drunk, whose divorce was one of several unmentionable secrets of Ocker Hill. Beyond him a hump-backed bridge crosses the canal. That is a boundary. To go further would be to venture into the hinterland that leads to Wednesbury. We three boys did not go there.

Had you turned the other way, closing the wooden gate behind you, you would have passed the same assortment of brick houses and passageways. One, much larger, leads to an open yard with stables. The Walkers live there. They are rich. Proof of their riches is the car on view in the yard, although no-one has seen it move. A short walk further – five minutes at most - and you arrive at a division of roads, many years later to be marked by a traffic island. At this point the railway line from the Power Station to Dudley Port passes under the road. Mr Gittens' little wooden newspaper shop is perched so directly over the tunnel that smoke billows in to mix with the smell of the pipe tobacco he dispenses from huge bottles on a shelf.

Mr Gittens' island is a boundary. Turn right, and you risk abandoning Ocker Hill, although no sign indicates the fact. Another road, almost parallel, arrives safely enough at St. Mark's church, passing Spring Street and the Methodist Chapel as you go. Turn left at this intersection of roads with Mr Gittens at your back, and you will be walking down the steep slope of Toll End Road to the village end. No toll to pay – the name is older by far than that. Beyond lies Great Bridge. Another place. We did not go there either.

There is a greengrocer in Toll End Road, and a clothes shop, usually shut. Spring Street has a bakers and a fish shop, wet by day and fried by night. At the foot of Toll End Road is the small Municipal Library I will read my way through when I grow up a bit. Beyond that, tarmac turns to dusty concrete and an estate of houses thrown up in hasty war-time months. Built where Moat Farm had stood for four hundred years or more, the houses have already started to crack. That place, the Lost City, was another and dangerous world. We certainly did not go there.

Apart from the *Crown and Cushion*, which is rather a grand public house, Leabrook Road has *The Railway Tavern*, crammed every night with singing, drinking, men. Not the contented Welsh miners of the newsreels, cheery faces decorated with a little coal dust, singing their hearts out in four-part harmony. The men of Ocker Hill bellow in demented unison to a piano apparently being beaten to death. I fall asleep each night to this lullaby and mind it far less than my mother did on my behalf. There was a third pub, *The Jolly Collier*, with just enough trade to limp along, but it was a surly, silent, place.

The house at number 160 was on the other side of the road, equidistant from these two pubs. Directly opposite, and separating them was a huge expanse of wasteland given over to rose bay willow herb. Not yet, but when I turned seven and could go out on my own, this field of purple flowers would become my first private paradise. For the moment, ignore the concrete bomb shelter in front. People did go in there, the smell was proof enough of that, but we never did, my brothers and I. It will soon be knocked down anyway and carted away, huge blocks of crumbling concrete trailing iron reinforcing rods, economy grade.

Ocker Hill is a divided place with choices to make: Church or Chapel; Wednesbury side or Great Bridge side; rowdy *Tavern* or silent *Collier*; the village or the Lost City. Choices that will determine your position in a class war fought with incredible ferocity. Mother and Father made their decision. She bought hake from the Spring

Street fishmonger, leaving the cod for poor people. Father bought *The Daily Express*, leaving *The Daily Mirror* for the poor. Mother was a teacher. Father, albeit a working man, wore a trilby hat.

Chapter 2

I must have spent time in the Ocker Hill Infants' School, but I have virtually no memory of the place. Apart, that is, from scratching letters on my slate in a vast gas-lit room, crammed with desks; every morning a new letter. We copied from an oilcloth roll suspended in front of the blackboard, each hieroglyph letter in lurid red cursive script. This arbitrary task, imposed without explanation, defined itself as mysteriously unattainable. There was also something about it that frightened me: I think it was the way the tips of each letter were decorated with little coloured flourishes, impossible to reproduce on slate.

I recall what must have been the morning of my arrival at this my first real school, sitting in lonely misery on a flight of stone steps in front of the entrance doors. An event the more dismal because it had been Mother herself who had abandoned me that morning, pressing a little paper packet of marmalade sandwiches into my hands. In her defence, she probably assumed I knew what all this was about; why I had been brought to this alien place with its iron gates; why I was to be surrounded by children I did not know; why I was alone.

The morning's slatework left the sandwiches so crushed I had to peel them apart, but eating them I recall gazing down on the sunlit buildings of Mother's pre-fab school, a lost arcadia. The memory must be false - it was impossible to see one school from the grounds of the other. Nonetheless, the taste of those sandwiches lives with me even now as a personal truth. I was, in a word, unhappy, my infant mind filled with waking dreams of an idyllic former life as an accidental interloper in Mother's "reception class." I can only imagine I decorated one of these dreams with marmalade.

Playtime in the Infants' School was spent in an asphalt yard milling with children. Stuart had possibly already graduated to the Primary School: I cannot recall seeing him. Since I had only played with my brothers up to that time, I never summoned up courage

11

to play with anyone else. I spent my time watching. In particular, watching girls, a completely novel breed of person, identified by their clothes. These were the days of the war-time "clothing coupon" in which boys wore trousers that inched their way higher as the year progressed, ending well above the knees. Girls wore colourless miniature reproductions of their mother's home-made dresses, but they too came with a tuck to let out in the spring. These strange beings had their own playground, separated from mine by a low wall on which I would sit to watch, their privileged apartness sufficiently exciting to keep me there. Apart from skipping (Father had forced me to acknowledge by then that boys did not skip), they chiefly engaged in two activities. I suppose the first of these might be described as *conversation*, although the word does not do justice to a sound more like the chattering of birds. They stood in circles of four or five, close enough for the exclusion of rivals, and shouted in overlapping monologues, pausing only to laugh. The second activity was more engaging. It involved pitching themselves into a kind of handstand against a wall, often ten or more upside-down girls at a time. To satisfy some modest impulse, or possibly because of my relentless surveillance, dresses were tucked in.

Sex wormed its way to the classroom more blatantly in my final year. A cupboard at the front of the room, next to the teacher's desk (the room contained little else by way of furniture) held sufficient dusty costumes to act out the drama of *The Sleeping Beauty*. This unpretentious weekly performance, with a cast of two, and only one of those standing, was played out with alphabetic regularity. Long before my turn arrived I had seen enough of the plot to know its denouement, and the inexorable approach of *K* brought me many a sleepless night. Decked out in my small green tabard, armed only with my scabbard, the sword having been mislaid somewhere, I was compelled to deliver that excruciating awakening kiss.

*

The Primary School in Ocker Hill was held in a single storey building in Spring Street, built from the same gloomy bluestone as the church of St. Mark which owned it. Not quite eight years old, I would walk there each day, navigating roads where horse manure and the beasts that produced it were a greater risk than cars. Since Father refused to give me a real one, I would stop on the way to light my imaginary cigarette, huddled against a wall cupping my hand against the wind. I smoked as I walked, only casting the fag end nonchalantly aside at the Boys School gate.

Since the school belonged to St. Mark, at least one day each week was set aside for instruction by Vicar Bell. He did little to temper his Christian apologetics to what was a largely heathen congregation, taking it on himself to prepare all pupils for the Anglican Communion, whether they liked it or not. Whatever the weather, in full ecclesiastical rig, including an odd octagonal black hat, he would crocodile us the hundred yards from school to church. An interminable hour later he would bring us back. Unlike most of these short-trousered parishioners I already knew the church well. On war-time winter Sundays, Stuart had been sent off to Matins in pitch dark clutching his torch with its enviable blue beam (to fox the passing German planes). After breakfast, Ian was formally placed in my charge for the walk to church for Morning Eucharist, each of us clutching our threepenny bit for the plate (cockney slang never having reached Ocker Hill, we blithely called it so). More often than not Ian escaped my grip, but neither of us escaped the weekly procession to Sunday Evensong organised by Father like a military parade, elders in their stiff best, little ones cleaned and pressed. Even school caps as these, progressively, came to hand. We were encouraged to feel slightly set apart from the rest of the village children: slightly, and absurdly, a little superior.

By the time I arrived at Primary School, Stuart was on his way to Grammar School. We shall return to this mysterious academic progression; at the time, his spiritual progress concerned me more. He had graduated to the status of Altar Server and no longer sat with his brothers at Morning Eucharist, appearing instead from behind an impressive curtain, complete with his own red gown. St. Mark's was my first experience of sacred places. It defined Sunday as a day apart to such a degree that I recall the slight sense of sacrilege that God might agree to attend on a school day, even at the behest of Vicar Bell. Watching Stuart about his sacred rites each Sunday morning I kept envy at bay, too deeply in awe ever to imagine I would emulate him. Indeed, I was never received into the Anglican Church, lapsing like Adam Bede into Methodism, albeit for scandalously irreligious reasons.

Primary School was where, finally, I graduated from slate to pen. Twice a week a rather disreputable person, smelling strongly of what I now know to have been beer, arrived to fill the two little china inkwells in each desk from a huge purple bottle. His name was Mr Turpin and for a long time I assumed he was the man himself or, at the very least, some highwayman-relative. My life thereafter was much concerned with nibs, curved copper things that slipped into a sheath on the pen. I was slow to master the art of dipping and my nib invariably shed a watery stream of blue-black liquid across the desk in its journey to the paper. We copied from different, and more complicated, oilskin rolls, writing on tiny stapled booklets of War Economy paper so thin that it tolerated only downward strokes of the nib. At that time I had the daily task of carrying home a loaf of bread from the shop at the foot of Spring Street. The bread invariably arrived blue at one end and tasting faintly of iron.

Theology consumed Thursday morning of each school week, the afternoon being given over to stories, I assume as consolation. I had not been read to before and these afternoons were my induction into another, magical, world. I recall in my second year (indeed, it is all I recall) a shaft of sunshine from the glazed rectangle of glass over the door singling out my desk, a tall woman, dark hair tied high in a bun, reading Mole's reflections on *home*, the book held out in one hand, fifty children in sleepily spellbound silence:

> He stopped dead in his tracks, his nose searching hither and thither in its efforts to recapture the fine filament, the telegraphic current, that had so strongly moved him. A moment, and he had caught it again; and with it this time came recollection in fullest flood. Home! That was what they meant, those caressing appeals, those soft touches wafted through the air, those invisible little hands pulling

14

and tugging, all one way! Why, it must be quite close by him at that moment, his old home that he had hurriedly forsaken and never sought again, that day when he first found the river!

*

Although she did her best to hide it, by the age of seven it was clear to all I was Mother's favourite, the next best thing to the girl-child she had always craved. No great imposition for me, since it did not take me long to discover the fate of the middle child of three brothers. Almost invariably, your older brother will look beyond you for companionship. Stuart and Ian made an unlikely pair. Nonetheless - more often than not - while they went roaming god knows where, I would find myself playing cards with Mother. It was when she began to teach me to knit, I first discovered the guilty pleasures of subversive activity. Along with skipping, Father strongly disapproved of knitting, considering both unmanly. But Mother's invisible little hands had begun to tug, offering me advantages I would have been wise to refuse. But who is wise at seven? Faced with an artless little face asking, *but why Daddy?* Father was powerless. Mother knew the game I was playing, and unwisely let me recruit her to this defiance. It was a tacit conspiracy that sowed the seeds of a lifetime of discord.

Among the many hours spent with Mother in these dangerous girls' games, the most memorable was a year-long theatrical venture. We set out to make a troupe of *papier mâché* puppets' heads from newspaper soaked in flour and water. The intention had been to construct the complete cast of a Punch and Judy show with knitted bodies stuffed with cotton wool. Alas, apart from the crocodile, all the characters, when painted, came out looking like Punch, even with my own knitted jackets (pearl and plain, with Mother "casting off"). Stuart helped me construct a theatre from a cardboard box begged from the grocers and large enough to stand inside. Tickets were printed and sold for puppet shows that took place in the blackout kitchen, the auditorium lit with candles perched in saucers of water. Father refused to be defined as any part of my audience but eventually agreed to attend in a technical role, standing at the back with a bowl of water in case of fire. Eventually, his official ARP electric torch was offered as extra stage lighting.

*

I spent a great deal of time in Primary School day-dreaming. Given his work ethic, Sigmund Freud was surprisingly charitable to day-dreamers, possibly because he counted himself as one and eventually put the practice to therapeutic ends, re-naming it *psychoanalysis*. I doubt I could have afforded his fees, which is a pity, because my case - which was not at all out of the ordinary - merited his interest. I was, by choice, a somewhat solitary child and Primary School, much to my surprise, found me perpetually fearful. Indulge me if I try to explore the reasons. I think it must have been in my second year that I discovered how few of my classmates understood – still less shared - my parents' views on the purposes of education. For Mother, education patently defined itself as a public good, as an end in itself. Her boast was that no child left her class unable to read. The fact that virtually all her pupils were destined to leave school aged fourteen, translating themselves into instant miniature adults, she considered a national scandal. Unfortunately, only a tiny minority of the hundreds she taught shared her view.

A proposal to raise the leaving age to fifteen had been shelved for the duration of the war, but the post-war Labour government made it the law. Already suspicious of the fraud at the heart of the enterprise that was blighting their days, my classmates did not welcome this extra year of bondage. To my mother's dismay, I was to be raised among a generation of cynics: boys whose brothers had been sitting in these self-same desks not so long ago and now worked for a living. These miniature men caught their daily bus to the Patent Shaft factory in overalls, none would have been seen dead in short trousers. My fellow pupils looked on this enviable generation as creatures from a golden age in which it was easily possible to save enough for a motorbike. Little wonder our overcrowded roomful of feckless urchins passed its time plotting their own escape.

They were not to know, of course, that I had already beaten them to it, spending my days in a private moonbeam world. An obedient little chap, I was stationed at the back of the room with the clever boys and left to dream my days away, only waking now and then to complete some entirely inconsequential task. My playmates of that time were - to the last animal - entirely fictional. I could say they came from somewhere else, but in truth I had already followed them to wherever it was and knew the place better than anywhere you might call reality. Eventually Mother explained I was too old for Muffin the Mule and must soon bid farewell to Rupert the Bear. I was sorry to let Rupert go, having spent a year clipping his daily exploits from a newspaper and pasting them into a book, but William Brown fast became an entirely acceptable replacement in subversive prose that served me well beyond my Primary days. The Swallows and the Amazons followed shortly after, then Jennings, Biggles, Bunter and many another.

The downfall of this dreamy child living in worlds remote from Ocker Hill was, of course, inevitable. It deserves a title that somehow Conan Doyle overlooked: *The Case of the Contested Gas Monitor*. On dark winter mornings we would arrive to find four massive gas lamps high above our heads already lit, filling the room with a sulphurous farty smell and an uncertain fluttering greenish light. Beneath each glass globe there were little outstretched copper arms and at some predetermined moment the chosen child of the day was allowed to take a pole from its place in the corner, reach up, and pull down the arms of each lamp in turn. To be Gas Monitor was to be a kind of King bringing daylight to his subjects. Better than that – in winter, as evening approached, the process reversed, flaring the lamps into brilliant life with satisfying minor explosions.

I had been anticipating my own brief reign for weeks. As with the regrettable business of the green tabard, the alphabet played a part and I waited my turn. That particular late afternoon was gratifyingly gloomy and at the customary, *Who's next with the gas?* I sprang up. Incredibly, another boy – although surely there was no other *K*? - popped up as well. We stood viciously eyeing each other across the room, until the teacher's casual airy wave in my direction set my downfall in train.

And it was not long coming. The following morning, I arrived to find two boys at the school gate - towering brutish hulks, they must have been all of ten years old. They let me by, pushing me on my way, but when I glanced back they were blocking the way for others who had followed me up Spring Street, shoving them towards the gate for the girls. I turned the corner leading to the entrance doors to be met by a group of boys, the sheepish-looking rejected gas monitor among them. It was not this *K minor* standing on the lowest step of the entrance confronting me, but their chosen champion, a lanky boy with floppy hair, surveying the mob like Nero in his pomp. Oddly, they seemed to be jeering this tall stranger as they pushed me towards him from behind. It was only when I had been prodded uncomfortably close that I realised the jeering was meant for me. Realisation dawned as someone pushed me from behind, pitching me hard against the lanky boy.

Even without the help of the lower step this giant was far taller than me. He fell back, grunting a little, as I landed head-first low down in the pit of his stomach. A howl of denunciation rose from behind me, somewhat in the style of a Greek chorus: *That's a foul, that is… stomach's a foul … you've a right to do it back,* and so on. I couldn't make it all out because in executing my unintended head butt I had bitten my lip and drips of blood were already staining the front of my shirt. We both stepped back, he a step up to higher ground, me temporarily to join the chorus. No seconds were on hand with sponges but a definite pause settled on the proceedings. I risked a timid upward glance. My adversary, framed in his doorway and no longer winded, was sizing me up for round two. I have no idea what devil drove me at that exact moment – perhaps it was the look in his eye - but I flung myself upon his lower parts, arms flailing like a demented threshing machine, ineffectual little hands flapping at his legs. Mad with rage certainly, but dimly conscious that dreadful retribution was at hand. And I was correct. Something out of my vision seemed to deflect my assailant's intended blow. As my efforts exhausted themselves in diminishing spasms, a force greater than I thought possible seemed to bear me aloft. I was left dangling by my trouser belt like a gaffed fish, my face closer than it ever should have been to the tobacco-stained moustache of God himself. My opponent, his pose no less undignified, dangled from the other hand.

You rarely saw the Headmaster of St. Mark's Primary. He led us in morning prayers, more vengeful than Vicar Bell's, but otherwise occupied his hours meting out justice with a long wicker cane. I had prayed never to see the room where all this took place – it had been enough to hear – but my nightmares had left me familiar with the place nonetheless. An expansive space, I thought, groaning with books, but room enough to wield the cane. It was a disappointment, this shabby little den smelling of pipe tobacco, crumpled scraps of paper on a carpet not much bigger than the desk. And not a single book.

I could feel that the boy at my side was consumed with terror. He had been here before. You got three for fighting, I recalled, although the tariff had not been written down. Perhaps it was six. All I seemed to know was it came in multiples of three. He was pressing both his hands hard against his side as a ritual prophylactic. Yes, he had been here before.

Our tormentor squeezed past to his desk, dropping into a curious chair that swivelled round. The cane – shorter than I had imagined – lay on a pile of papers. He reached out towards it, but only to tap his pipe against a little china dish. The pipe finally stuffed with tobacco, he struck a match. We watched in awestruck silence as it burned itself out round his fingers. He seemed not to notice.

Who started it?

'E did.

He struck another match turning his gaze on me, the flame creeping on.

That right?

Any plausible response would demand more than this particular advancing flame would permit and I settled for a simplifying nod. In any case, my voice had long since gone. He lit the pipe, waited until the cloud of blue smoke seemed dense enough, then pointed its stem at the other boy, waving him out of the room. A profound silence followed the patter of his retreating steps. My racing heart gauged at least an hour's worth of aromatic smoke. It may have been less, but certainly enough to reflect on what Mother would say about my shirt.

You started it?

19

It was a while before I realised he had spoken. Not quite the same voice this time, more conversational, more the kind that in better worlds normal people use. Normal enough to reply had I the use of my voice, but it was far too late for that. Even the will to nod had drained away and I lifted my head for one last despairing glance. And then it was, he smiled.

No ordinary smile. A smile that came to punctuate my life.

Let me say at once, there was nothing benevolent about this smile, no measure of regret in the fleeting expression that suggested my incautious glance had caught him unawares. He looked away, dissolving himself in a haze of pipe smoke, irritated. I sensed he knew I had seen more than I should in that secret little smile. A smile intended for himself and not for me. Sensed perhaps that I had caught a glimpse, if only for a fraction of a second, of a curtain pulled aside. A terrified little boy transfixed by the intricate turning cogs of a machine he was never meant to see. And even as I let my gaze fall I remembered the morning of the broken glass, remembered that it had been better not to know what Stuart knew. There had been conspiracy afoot that morning. There was more to the world than I thought – more even than I would want to know. It was much the same now, staring down at the pattern on this shabby bit of carpet: I did not know why I knew, but I knew as surely as anything that the wicker cane would lie untouched on the desk. The smile was still there as he pointed his pipe to the door, willing me out of the room.

As I made my way back to the classroom my adversary was waiting, all passion spent.

You geroff?

I managed a smile of my own.

Chapter 3

I was not to know it, but mine was the last generation of the scholars of Ocker Hill to fulfil the role of Gas Monitor. Buried among the many mysteries of that enigmatic smile lay the fact that Father had undertaken to wire the whole school for electricity in the summer holiday between my third and final year. Not perhaps the most propitious time for the Headmaster to send a blood-stained son home with smarting hands. On such unknowns are battles won.

To my delight, I was recruited that summer as Electrician's Assistant. Not Father's first choice, but Stuart, elevated to his new school and dressed accordingly, was now above such things and Ian was too small. I threw myself into the world of manual labour with an enthusiasm that even Father must have found embarrassing. The job had to be done in his free time, after work, so each day he would find me waiting at the kitchen door, torch in hand. Each day, at his command, I would crawl with suicidal zeal into increasingly inaccessible recesses beneath the classroom floors. And each day now, spectacularly dirty, I would help gather up the scattered tools to make the journey home, walking at his side down Spring Street, for all the world like a plumber and his dusty mate.

The work involved tracing an intricate pattern of six-foot lengths of threaded iron conduit, working room by room, first under the floor, then along walls and ceilings to service massive electric globes. The church provided the materials but Father donated his labour, bequeathing to St. Mark's Primary School an electrical supply that easily outlived the building and the advent of the "ring" circuit. It also laid the groundwork for Mother's all-too-brief theatrical career.

During the week the fast-retreating daylight left us little time for talk, but weekends were different. No longer restricting himself to barking, *pass me that*, Father began to unburden himself of a lifetime of frustrations and thwarted ambitions. I was not the audience he would have chosen for these mumbled monologues, but I did my best,

21

sitting silently as bitter words washed over my uncomprehending head. Trained as a City and Guilds electrical engineer, he had dismissed as demeaning the prospect of a life spent mending kettles and opted for the more romantic alternative of maintaining power lines. He was an ardent supporter of the Scout movement and the outdoor life suited him. In any case, there was undeniable prestige attached to the men who climbed the massive pylons. Nonetheless, it was an unlucky choice: it would not be long before a primitive television set appeared in every house and electricians prospered. It was unlucky in another way, because the onset of war found other, more urgent, uses for Father's skills. He was drafted to work as part of a team of engineers maintaining the independent power station serving the vast ICI complex at Oldbury. A reserved occupation, it was as dangerous as anything he might have met in combat since the place manufactured high explosives and was regularly bombed, but being exempted war service left him feeling irrationally guilty. A tiny sepia photograph tucked into the corner of the mantel shelf mirror served as atonement: his smiling younger brother, togged out in the uniform of the Merchant Navy. Uncle Arthur survived the war but the trauma of service on the North Atlantic convoys had left him unemployable. Already stricken with irrational guilt, Father was forced to watch his brother settle to life in a rented house in Toll End Road with little more than the use of a cold water tap and access to a communal lavatory.

To Mother's horror it was while serving my time as apprentice electrician that I became aware of another, and darker, Ocker Hill. In particular, its heretical alternative religious tradition, Methodism. Unable to pass my days playing in the neighbouring fields, high summer brought the first encounter with a Procession of Witness. No tottering Madonna, of course, and certainly no melancholy Verdi, but an annual display of Methodist paganism quite exotic enough to justify Mother's worst imaginings. In particular, there were banners - condemned as papist flummery (theology was not Mother's strong suit). Some, in fact were old enough to have welcomed John Wesley himself, faded embroidered relics exhumed from the coal cellars of Ocker Hill. Others were gaudy things borrowed from chapels as far away as Toll End and Gospel Oak. All supplemented by Trade Union banners of a plausibly spiritual character.

On *Walking Day*, as the locals called it, a flock of chattering girls in white, having concluded their heathen Methodist rites, streamed through the chapel doors to pass two awestruck electricians at the gates of the school. Down Spring Street, past our house in Leabrook Road (although certainly Mother did not watch), to disappear into the maze of featureless streets beyond the canal bridge. Led by Ocker Hill's sole defender of the peace, devout Methodist to his core and solemnly cradling his helmet in his arms, half a mile or more of bedraggled humanity snaked by at the pace of the slowest walking infirm: children too hot in their best clothes; decorated prams with bawling babies; barking dogs; women with sticks; little boys with bicycles too precious to leave behind. And girls. Girls in white. Girls everywhere. Even when they could no longer be seen, the distant sound of a huge bass drum marked their way: BOOM BOOM, BOOM, pausing now and then to let the Boys' Brigade deliver bugle accounts of parade ground calls, the only tunes they knew.

An hour later, the caravan would reappear in Toll End Road steered on its unsteady way by Chapel Elders, over-dressed and sweating in the sun, armed with collecting boxes. Wooden things, shaken like football rattles at onlookers on doorsteps; at faces behind lace curtains; even - since its purpose had sanctified the day – at the residents of the smoky snug bars of forbidden pubs reeking of Saturday's beer. Back at the Chapel, urns of tea for the grown-ups waited on trestle tables with cakes for the children, although not the sort with icing, this being Sunday. Consumed in silence in a downstairs room to the sound of the wooden boxes shaken out in the vestry upstairs. There was just about time for a rushed dinner before the chapel pews were packed for the Anniversary Service. Shockingly, even people from church went to that, even me (although not that year), inevitably wondering whether it was permitted to sing the curiously enthusiastic hymns, or indeed any hymns, given they were in the wrong book. Father was a Church Warden at St. Mark's and, for him, this tendency to fall into vulgar display typified all that was wrong with Methodism. He even asked the vicar to devise a march as a more sober rejoinder. But the Church Calendar was against them, the first and only attempt defeated by relentless rain: St. Mark's feast falls in April, no time to be parading in Ocker Hill.

Thoughts of girls in white kept me awake in bed that night. Some I knew by sight from school, although never dressed that way. Thoughts I had never entertained before left me pleasurably musing on dresses not always quite long enough. And on legs. I had never much considered legs until then. One girl in particular, taller than the rest and with legs to match, quite grown up in fact. This rounded goddess, shepherding a group of infants past where we stood, turned to wave a white-gloved hand, catching my eyes with hers. I sensed Father looking down at my scalding face, but he did not ask who she was.

*

The rent of 160, Leabrook Road was 10/3d, the sum to be placed weekly into the hands of Mrs Harrison our landlord's wife, a tiny woman, almost as wide as she was tall. She rarely moved from her kitchen chair and it was there I would meet her every three weeks when it was my turn with the money. Mother arranged the rent book with a ten-shilling note folded inside and gave us the coin to hold, but if she hoped we would return clutching a threepenny bit she was invariably disappointed. At the due hour, the Harrison's formidable garden gate, set into a high wall, was unlocked and left a little ajar. Beyond, was a formal garden, complete with sweeping lawns, terraced flowerbeds, heated greenhouses and, almost always, Mr Harrison himself, standing guard. In the mood, he would waylay you for a conducted tour of his boiler house, a spectacular coke-fired affair that kept the greenhouses in tropical heat, even in winter. The Harrisons were not the sort to let anything so trivial as war spoil their orchids; neither were bureaucratic restrictions going to deprive them of the coke for the furnace. Whence came this coke was a question best not posed. Father claimed he knew, but rented houses in Ocker Hill were hard to come by and he kept his peace.

He was a romantic character, our landlord, old beyond his years, like a rakish version of Sir Edward Elgar, with a shaggy tobacco-stained moustache. He chain-smoked a succession of cigarettes from a packet bearing a bearded picture of Uncle Arthur framed by a lifebelt - Players Navy Cut, each one lit with the stub end of its predecessor. It did not take us long to discover Father disapproved of Mr Harrison, refusing to have anything to do with rent, rent book, or threepenny bits. Not that this was any kind of inconvenience to we three boys. We looked forward to our weekly encounters, considering him the closest to a pirate we were likely to encounter in land-locked Ocker Hill, adopting him as the grandfather who had somehow escaped us. For his part, the pirate rather enjoyed his reputation, letting us in on various bits of minor adult delinquency. I recall his displaying a tap artfully concealed in a hollowed-out rock in one of the flower beds, explaining to three goggle-eyed little boys that this was the supply of special water on which his paradise depended. He must have installed it himself as the houses were being built, ensuring the pipework knew nothing of the water meter. His secret was safe with the Musketeers.

The outbreak of war had brought an end to domestic pets, although Mrs Harrison's plump Labrador - called Poll or some such name – miraculously escaped the necessary cull. She was never seen beyond their garden gate, although I woke one night to find her standing at my bedside noisily nuzzling my hand. Bedroom doors were not kept closed after the era of night-time raids and she must have negotiated her way through the maze of cellars in search of playmates. She stood looking at me for a while, her breath smelling of hot liver, then padded her way downstairs.

To my surprise, when I told this story to Mother in the morning, she roundly declared it nonsense; I had certainly been dreaming. She waited until Father came into the room to say he should be ashamed to see what playing with electricity had brought me to. It was unnatural for a boy. Putting me to crawling about under floors had made me feverish, I should be out in the sun, not pining for dogs. As she pushed me aside, I realised she had seen my days with Father as a betrayal and was taking revenge. Nonetheless, the look on Father's face when she said I was pining for a dog stayed with me. She knew well enough I was not given to pining, but the curious association began to do its work. Fragments of memory slowly pieced themselves into a pattern hovering between reality and fiction. One Christmas in particular, the memory muddled in with the smell of turkey and the sight of presents set out on a table I was too small to reach. There had been a puppy - small, black, disconcertingly mobile, chewing at newspapers Stuart had laid on the kitchen floor.

That remote Christmas Day comes, even now, flavoured with a desperate sense of loss. It was bitterly cold and Ian cried at being left behind. I trailed on aching legs behind Stuart down Doe Bank Road between looming walls of shovelled snow calling the puppy's name until we had gone further than I had ever been. An alien place, the sun no more than feeble yellow light, almost gone. As we turned back, Stuart stood to call a final time. Mother said we should not fret, it had been her present, after all, and the dog could find its own way home. But she had forgotten its name and I remember Father looked away. Much as he turned away now to busy himself with nothing very much.

*

I am in bed, wide awake, heart drumming. Downstairs they are bickering like the days when Ian wet the bed. I go back to my prayers, adding one that God would make them stop, but God fails to intervene and they take turns to shout, trading words like players in an angry tennis match, Father barking to stem the flow of Mother's voice. A door bangs and I know he has shut himself in the kitchen and she starts crying to fetch him back. I hear his voice muttering *shush you'll wake the children* and lie in the breathless silence listening to my heart, wondering whether she is crying still, until I fall asleep, only to wake to furious whispered shushing sounds seeping through the wall from their bedroom. They have come upstairs, Mother forgetting to be quiet, shouting *it's that Connie Fately isn't it?* I have never heard this name before and I don't like the *Fately* part – it doesn't sound like anybody's name. Father is pleading *give it a rest Dot, for God's sake, you'll wake the children.* Then it's Mother's turn, quieter, but loud enough to hear: *you tell that to your fancy woman, tell it your Connie then, you tell her that.*

Stuart found out who Connie was before me. It was in a yellow book Mother had wrapped in sugar paper to keep it clean. I asked her what it was and she said it was a play called *Poison Pen* and she had to learn it off by heart because she had to act in it. She read it with Stuart in the kitchen, but she said he mangled the words. But at least I knew that Connie Fately, the fancy woman, was somebody in a play. She committed suicide Mother said, and good riddance, which made Father laugh then say *give it a rest*. She asked him if he would call her Phryne because that's the name in the play and that would help, but he says *help what?* and won't call her anything because the name was silly. But he took the book off Stuart, all the same, and went with her into the kitchen. And we sit listening to awkward muffled words through the closed door.

Father must always have intended a theatrical dimension to his wiring scheme because we returned to school that year to find an impressive gantry of spotlights high in the ceiling of the schoolroom. That, and three mammoth rheostats locked behind a cupboard with glass doors. But we had yet to discover all that – first came the three nights when St. Marks' Amateur Dramatic Society performed *Poison Pen*, on a stage fashioned from planks laid across the children's desks. We were seated with Stuart in the middle, in the front row, watching Mother in the play. A demonic mother we barely recognised hounding Connie Fately to her suicide: she hanged herself, although there was only a shadow to watch. After the final performance I stood alongside Father in a room smelling hot and greasy filled with men too big to notice me. A tall woman in a green dress pushed past to get to where Father was standing. She rested her hand on my head for a second, turning it into a tiny rap of knuckles and murmuring *so this is the little chap*? I looked up and saw Father nod. He looked unhappy, glancing down at me. I wanted to say something, but could think of nothing to say. Then Mother appeared, still wearing the clothes from the play and the woman backed away. I never saw her again.

*

It must have been a few days later. I am in the kitchen, standing next to the dresser with the front pulled down to make a little table. Outside, it is a sunny afternoon, the snow making everywhere too light. Father is in the living room reading his newspaper, his feet perched up on a chair, smoke from his cigarette drifting into the kitchen. Mother is pouring him a cup of tea from the pot with brown and yellow bands. There are two cups, side by side, but she is only pouring into one of them. It suddenly strikes me that she is standing too still, her head rigid, holding the pot too high, not looking at it. I watch as the cup fills and overflows into the saucer then spills out across the shelf of the dresser to splash down onto the floor. She is still pouring; still holding the pot; still standing rigidly upright, her back stiff. I run into the living room to fetch father, but find myself unable to speak and stand there looking at him as he puts the newspaper aside.

That must have been the winter of 1947. A cold winter and me barely eight. A bad year to catch epilepsy - because that was what had befallen Mother, not that it was something you catch, the doctor said – it was more a random affliction of the mind, appearing and disappearing to a calendar of its own devising. You could see he had decided to be kind, this bustling little man, to put in a special effort for the children sitting in the front room. Father had lit a fire for the occasion filling the air with smoke from the shovel of hot coals he had brought from the living room. The doctor pretended to be talking to Mother but turned to Stuart now and then, using a different voice to say we should not be frightened. Which was frightening because we didn't know why we were there, why father had silently stationed himself a little apart, endlessly twisting a bit of wire in his hands. We must wait to see if it reappeared, the doctor said, nodding as if he'd guessed when Father said it already had. In that case, we must wait again, to see whether the seizures became more frequent. He asked Stuart whether he understood the word. It was called an *Absence Seizure*. Apparently, Mother simply went away for a while, although we can see she's still there.

For we three children that was the start of a new life with Mother, one in which we would be left behind. A life in which Mother herself would almost never be fully well and would, over the course of many years, inexorably mutate into someone else altogether. As a foretaste, and to the dismay of Vicar Bell, she abandoned St. Mark's church for the pages of *Prediction* magazine. The herbal remedy she had bought at Wednesbury market all those years before had been prepared by a woman content to call herself a witch and although Methodist Ocker Hill had disowned its pagan past, there were still those willing to see epilepsy as a uniquely diabolical affliction. Not so much a disease in the natural way of things, but a curse that had emerged, unasked in Mother's case, from a nexus of issues: her hounding the fictional Connie Fateley to her suicide; her fantastical elaboration of Father's relationship with the woman who took that part; memories of her own attempted suicide years before. Perhaps, if Father had heeded the doctor's words, she might, in time, have regained a semblance of normality. But Father could not wait - he had demons of his own to contend with. His increasingly desperate search for a cure began that week with Mother's first prescription for phenobarbital, a drug which succeeded in replacing temporary periods of absence with something altogether more permanent.

Chapter 4

The 1944 Education Act envisaged free secondary education for all pupils, with specialised provision for academic or technical high-flyers. The pupils of St. Mark's School were enthusiastically prepared for the annual "eleven-plus" examinations which would determine their academic future. Father had long since determined that Stuart would fly high enough and had settled on his becoming a doctor, a somewhat quixotic decision given it would involve the expense of a university education - his own life decisions had ensured his family would have many desirable things, but money would never be among them. It was the onset of Mother's epilepsy which cemented his ambition: the certainty of some future cure was to rest on Stuart's imminent secondary education. So far as I know, Stuart's views on this question were not sought. He had never shown the slightest interest in science and spent most of his time producing remarkable drawings from life. He was probably born to be an artist, but Father had no time for ideological niceties and was more concerned with the formidable practical obstacles which stood in his way. The chief among these was also the most obvious - there was no grammar school within reasonable range of the inhabitants of Ocker Hill and never had been; it had never crossed anyone's mind that a demand might exist. There were plans to build a grammar school in Tipton, but the lethargic planning for that had yet to find somewhere suitable to build it. Which left but one alternative - a rather forbidding establishment ten miles away, in a different county, and decidedly reluctant to admit the children of the poor. Given all this, it might seem miraculous that Stuart came to attend King Edward VI Grammar School in Stourbridge and I can only offer a small piece of (surely apocryphal) family history as to how it came about. We were told that a certain *Uncle Tom*, a distant relative of Mother's, albeit someone we were destined never to meet, had contacted the school and told them that Stuart's remarkably high marks in the eleven-plus examination entitled him to a place. Far more likely it was the work of Mother's sister, Bessie, who by then had married well, to someone with connections in the labyrinthine politics of the Midlands. Apparently, there are strings to be pulled in the most egalitarian of worlds and my brother did, indeed, take the first steps that year on the long road which led him to a Fellowship of the Royal College of Surgeons.

Three years later it was my turn, although I was still only ten when I took the eleven-plus examinations, my birthday falling on the first of October. I subjected myself to a series of hour-long tests in arithmetic and English composition with the added bonus of tests in non-verbal and verbal intelligence. Taken in a state of such contented insouciance that I have but one memory of the event: the oddity of being taken to a vast hall filled with the bowed heads of earnest children and ordered to write an essay on trains.

When the results were declared, I had done well enough to be defined as the second of Father's high-flying sons and learned, for the first time, of his ambition that I was to become a scientist. Pressed to define this occupation he was disappointingly vague. Perhaps he had been impressed by my brief period as amateur electrician. I can think of no other reason why he should sit me down one afternoon and solemnly explain that I was to embark on an apprenticeship. I found the very word intimidating and was horrified to learn that it would involve my leaving home and sleeping in a dormitory. He had determined I would join a shadowy military establishment near Malvern to practise whatever apprentices did. He must have been hatching the scheme for some time because he was alarmingly well informed, proudly declaring that I would be working at the very place where radar had been invented. I recall being terrified, particularly by the prospect of the dormitory, but Mother explained that the proposal was really something for the future, I needed to be at least fifteen to enrol and I might well have changed my mind before then. The arrival of a letter a few days later spared my explaining that I had already changed it: by the application of a "keep families together" rule, I was to attend the same grammar school as Stuart.

My first day at King Edward's, Stourbridge involved my first bus journey of any sizable duration. At slightly over an hour, it seemed interminable. Although my new leather satchel had yet to contain anything, wild horses would not have parted me from it, so Mother strapped the hollow object to my back, making it almost impossible to sit comfortably. Fortunately, close observation of fellow scholars in the street during the five-minute pause in Dudley revealed that satchels were carried rather than worn that year and I wriggled out of it.

The bus deposited me directly outside the school and I was able to make my way up an impressive stone staircase. To encounter at the top someone I took to be a teacher on guard duty who asked me where my mother and father were. I mumbled some kind of inconsequential answer because in truth I had no idea where they were and she led me into a vast hall, walking a trifle too fast, in what I construed as a rather disapproving way. I was plonked into a seat near the back and left to survey the scene. Of those present, actual school pupils were so much a minority that they were barely visible. The place was filled with chattering adults – mothers and fathers, certainly, but also a fair smattering of uncles, aunts and elderly relatives who had come for the show. My arrival at the back interrupted a conversation which now continued over my head as I perched the precious satchel at my feet. A tall man in khaki uniform in the seat in front had craned round to talk to a motherly-looking woman seated at my side. Beyond her sat a small boy, patently as nervous as me, kitted out in jacket and cap as bright and new as my own. Both parties to this conversation were speaking at full volume so I had no alternative but to listen in and understand, at least to the degree that my over-heated imagination permitted. It went as follows:

Soldier - *Have you met the new man?*

Motherly Woman - *No, there was a meeting last night but he couldn't come.*

Soldier - *I couldn't either.*

Motherly Woman - *They say he's very young. I thought Frank Carter was to get the job.*

Soldier - *Old Cranky? No, they wanted a new broom. This chap's from Cambridge.*

Motherly Woman - *All these changes. It's a shame.*

Soldier - *Looks like they've sent old Carter to count the new ones.*
She - *Count the silver, more like. Tykes.*

A man had appeared on the stage in front of us as this conversation drew to a close. As the woman at my side had mentioned counting the silver she had glanced down at me in a less than motherly fashion. The soldier burst out laughing.

The man on the stage had come in through a door at the front of the hall, letting it bang behind him as a kind of request for silence. He cleared his throat, said good morning, and began calling out names from a list. Since the activity was close enough to counting, I concluded this must be Mr Carter and not the new broom. As each name echoed round the hall there was a pause until the appropriate little family group collected itself together and made its way outside. I could see them through the open door, bidding farewell to a succession of little boys identically clad in black coats with green piping at the sleeve.

As the alphabet progressed towards the letter K I became all too conscious that I was alone. Once outside, there would be no solicitous parents to guide me on my way, no mother to deliver a little departing kiss. Mr Carter was allocating boys in turn to groups he designated *alpha* or *beta*. If he kept to this regime, I calculated I could find the way by shadowing whoever had been sent out two letters ahead of mine. The relief as I arrived at this conclusion swiftly evaporated as I realised that the letter K had come and gone and we were already well into the Smiths. I sat on as the rows of chairs around me emptied. Sat on, in fact, until the families Williams and Young had noisily rattled their way out. I was left alone with Mr Carter.

I had seen *Great Expectations* and would not have been surprised to find myself strangely translated into Pip, stumbling into some alternative black-and-white universe at the command, *What name, boy?* I rescued my satchel and sat clutching it for consolation, feeling very small. But no one called. In fact, it was Mr Carter who came to me, his footsteps clicking military-style down the empty aisle, doing his best to smile as he arrived. He stood for a second then asked me my name, explaining that "Alan" was not quite enough. A glance at his list appeared to confirm that there had been no overlooked Kennedy and he asked for my address as a final resort. I rattled off, *160, Leabrook Road*, wisely adding *Ocker Hill* since he seemed to prefer the full version, but his frown only deepened. I might as well have said Timbuktu.

He took my hand, prised me up from my seat, and led me silently outside, across a courtyard, up a flight of stone steps, through a huge green door flung open, and down a corridor smelling of furniture polish. To stand at another door with a cracked wooden plaque reading, *Headmaster,* in ominous gilt letters. If I was indeed to be swept back home, here lived the new broom from Cambridge who would do the sweeping. The mysterious man with an inexplicable habit of counting silver. I suppose I should have been overwhelmed by the injustice of my predicament, but in truth I had more pressing concerns. I stood in increasing distress, first on one leg then the other, reflecting on my abandoned arcadia in Ocker Hill. In particular, how wonderfully accessible had been the lavatories of Saint Mark's Primary School. As these painful thoughts became ever more pressing a cheerful woman appeared at the door and coyly beckoned me inside with a crooked finger. Then she saw my anguished face. She had read that look before and, although we were yet to be introduced, the redoubtable Miss Bunn barely paused to seize my one available hand and hurry me away. It was a very grand lavatory, albeit one I was destined never to see again. Agreeably perfumed and mercifully close at hand, I recall a vast white basin with the word Shanks emblazoned in blue, and surprising soap that smelled of flowers.

Perhaps it was the fact that Miss Bunn had preserved her smile until I emerged, but my time sequestered in that little oasis had somehow broken a spell. The Headmaster knew all about me, she said, but they had been expecting me next year, not this. *So fancy that*, she added, and laughed. I was not to worry, they would fit me in, an extra desk was hardly a squeeze. Particularly when I'd come so far, managing another little laugh.

*

34

It was well past five when I brought my empty satchel home. On the journey back I had rehearsed a racy account of new school life for Mother, filled with Carters, Bunns, New Brooms and extra desks. She heard me out, forgetting to smile, even frowning a little when I mentioned tykes. But I could see she was barely listening, endlessly glancing down at the slip of paper I had pressed into her hand. I had read it on the bus. Nothing much, just a few lines setting out complicated new arrangements for my mid-day meal and who to give the money to for eating it. It seemed that most boys lived close enough to go home to eat their dinner but a remaining few, drawn, like Stuart, from remote locations, took sandwiches, and had fallen into the habit of eating them wherever they could find a spot. Faithful to the spirit of the 1944 Act, Mr Chambers, the new Headmaster, intended to bring this anarchic arrangement to an end, willing into being something altogether more formal. Alas, he was born too soon to shake off the comic potential of his unfortunate name - chamber pots still lurked beneath the beds of Stourbridge – and it was as "The Pot" he ordained that new boys who could not go home to eat, henceforth must eat a proper meal at a proper table. Until a canteen could be built, he said, the dining rooms of various masters would have to serve. How he had persuaded them into this hare-brained scheme must remain a mystery, but he was surely unaware of the domestic catastrophe it had called down on the benighted occupants of distant Leabrook Road. The costs of his well-intentioned civilising gesture were set out at the foot of the slip of paper: more than modest, given pudding was optional, but far beyond our means to pay. There was, of course, the other form which could be completed, but Mother would rather have eaten gruel herself than have a child of hers look to the State for its food.

I have no idea how the money was raised and strongly suspect someone went without, but for the ensuing several weeks, almost into winter, I joined a little group of sullen boys in the chilly dining room of a certain Mr Carpenter reluctantly to eat a meal I must learn to call *lunch*. His wife served at the table, having cooked what we ate. Similar groups were served by similar wives in other dining rooms scattered round the neighbourhood. Even I could see this mad Dickensian scheme could not endure and, one by one, boys found reasons, not always wholly truthful, as to why they should

35

be elsewhere. When Mrs Carpenter announced to the smattering of boys still left that she would be away on holiday for a week or more, we did not return and no one came looking.

I had imagined Mother would be relieved to learn I could now take sandwiches like Stuart, but to my surprise she resisted, asking why could I not join another group and gain entry to some other dining room? She had been proud of my daily visit to the Carpenters, quizzing me as much about the cutlery as the food. Sandwiches seemed suddenly to define a dangerous social decline. She agreed to prepare them only when I listed the members of the rather superior picnic party I had been invited to join, unaware that entry to this select club had been secured by trading the promise of her beef and pickled onion against some other boy's alien bread in an impromptu street market that sprang up each day in a corner of the playground.

A few days into the dawn of this new sandwich era I was sitting on a low wall in the playground waiting for the first of the two bells that signalled the start of the day. Saturday being a half day, there were no sandwiches to trade, although the insane rush for the bus that morning had meant there would have been none, whatever the day. Mother's attacks had returned. They did not last so long now, phenobarbital blurring the seizure into something not so very far from sleep, but were frightening nonetheless. Imagine she's taking a little nap, the doctor had said, but the way she ground her teeth seemed the opposite of sleep. That Saturday morning, she had seemed to know that an attack was on its way, suddenly stumbling across the kitchen to sit in rigid immobility in her chair. I went to take her hand but Stuart said that was no use and I would have time to catch the bus if I ran. He would stay and wait until Father came back from the shops, then catch the other bus to Great Bridge. He had done that before and the conductor let you use your pass, better he was late for school than me. As I made to run outside, he switched the wireless on and Mother opened her eyes, staring about as if unsure where the sound was coming from. I heard Stuart fill the kettle, telling her he would make her a cup of tea, but she had closed her eyes again and seemed not to hear. I pushed past Father at the door, calling back to him that Mother was having a turn and I would miss the bus, although people were still standing at the bus stop, so I had no need to run.

I waited on my wall until Stuart appeared in the playground just as the first bell rang. He waved, hurrying past a little group of boys, new like me, but from the other class. Something about my casual exchange with this unknown larger boy had seemed to provoke them and one of them let the others push him close to where I sat.

That your brother, then? You called Kendrick?

Kennedy.

Yes, Kennedy, that's right. I'm to tell you to see The Pot right away. Your Mother's dead.

It was a lie, of course, a brazen lie - the boy was trying to snare me into finding the green door locked. I knew the Headmaster didn't come on Saturday. I had seen Stuart cross the playground, flustered, but cheerful enough so it must have been a lie. Even this merciless child would not have grinned like that bearing news that Mother was dead. But the dreaded words had done their work, my heart pounding as wild imaginings chased through my head. What if Stuart had left before she died? But that would mean she really was dead. How could this boy know? How could anyone have known? Certain it was a lie, the truth of the words hung over me like an omen. The boy stepped awkwardly back to join the others, the grin no longer there, his face as white as mine. As they ran away he shouted I should learn to take a joke.

*

The second bell had rung before I found a master willing to hear my complicated complaint. I shall call him Major Delaunay here - it was his military rank, though not his name. He did not seem at all put out by the prospect of missing Assembly. All I knew of this mysterious man were stories brought back by boys daring enough to visit those distant parts of the school where all the teachers were men. A kind of composite Major Delaunay emerged from these witnesses: it was certain he had passed a dangerous war behind enemy lines; possibly he was an escaped prisoner of war, even now hunted by Nazis. He

37

taught French in the school, his romantic name confirming the fact, although he had also been heard speaking it, which clinched the matter. He was certainly a spy in disguise.

He listened to me in silence, frowning at the parts my Ocker Hill accent had rendered inaccessible. But translating the horror of my morning into coherent speech became increasingly difficult and I retreated into stifled sobs. He tossed what little was left of his cigarette to the ground, looking on incredulous as I did the best I could with my sleeve to wipe my nose. The stifled sobs were all I had. I increased the volume. *They don't do that here, you should know that.* He had a quiet measured voice like the man who read the news out on the wireless, and was certainly unaware how that single word *they* had lifted my heart, setting us apart, we two, against the baying mob.

What do you want me to do, then? What do you want? He caught the furtive glance towards the green door and shook his head. *No, you don't want that now, do you? Is he a big boy, this chap?* He smiled as I stammered no he was about as big as me – I had yet to learn the expression was school talk for a prefect. *Well, that's alright then. You know what I'd do in your place?* It wasn't really a question because he answered it himself, between efforts to light another cigarette. *I'd kick him in the slats. That's what I'd do. Now go away.*

Mother was cooking lamb chops for dinner when I got home. She told me to wash my hands then lay the table and go and find Ian. She didn't mention the seizure and I knew it was best not to ask.

Chapter 5

Stourbridge meant that for much of my school life I stood amid alien corn, a stranger in a strange land, facing choices not dissimilar to those my parents faced in Ocker Hill. But whereas it was always evident to them which way to jump (and to my brothers, come to that), some oddity of spirit left me rooted in indecision, with the result that I passed my childhood in two worlds, becoming something of a stranger in both. To explain how this came about takes me further than I meant to go, and even I accept this is far from explaining *why*, but bear with me if I abandon my chain-smoking French teacher for a while (fear not, Major Delaunay will return) and take you back five years or so.

I am standing unsteadily on a narrow wooden staircase, failing to take hold of an elaborate handrail just out of my reach, a terrifying procession of grown-ups pushing past me in both directions. People in their dozens, some up, some down, all too fast for me, calling and laughing to each other. Somewhere way above my head a man has started to sing in a tenor voice more powerful than anything you would ever hear in the pubs of Ocker Hill. Mother is there, standing below me beaming up from the turn of the stairs, her arms outstretched. Father, on the stair below, his arms clasped around her waist. Mother has mostly stopped smiling at home, but she is smiling now, calling to me. I have never seen the two of them happy together like this. She wants me to jump so she can catch me, but I am too frightened and sit down on the stairs, flinching as people step over me.

This memory has travelled well over seventy years. I was not yet six years old, in a Guest House in bombed-out Rhyl on the north coast of Wales. That was where holidays were spent and this was certainly a holiday because the war with Germany was finished. Fear of that war had consumed the few years I had accrued so far, with psychological consequences more enduring than the inconvenience of sleeping on folded rugs in a damp cellar in Leabrook Road. But

Father says we have won and that victory will make everything better. Of course, that was before he learned of another consequence altogether. Since Oldbury was no longer to be bombed, a grateful nation had released him from the hair-raising risks of his job and rendered him unemployed. I retain a tiny fragment of the memory of that, too. His coming into the kitchen with the letter, Mother taking it from his hand and sitting down to read it. Perhaps he said something. All I recall is feeling ashamed that I had seen him look like that. It was two long years before he found another job and he never knew my role in securing it.

*

That first winter of victory was bitterly cold and one morning the scholars of St. Mark's arrived at the school to be told the boiler had broken, there was no way of keeping them warm and they must go back home. To our delight we were released into the unwonted freedom of a frosty paradise. There was a pub on my way home and on days when the gates were left open for the horse-drawn dray, its garden provided a short-cut from Spring Street to Toll End Road. This was one such day. Although we had been ordered not to dawdle, with severe punishment for those who were late getting home, I knew there was no one waiting for me, so I dawdled to my heart's content, knowing Mother was at her school and Father would be working at one or another of the precarious jobs he had scraped into a livelihood.

The short-cut licensed a little exploration and I wandered into a spacious garden, walking between towering rows of raspberry canes, their dead leaves crisp with ice. To come face to face with a girl who seemed to have had the same idea. She was the daughter of our next-door neighbour, a year older than me. As a little girl she had played with the Kennedy boys, joining in the less boisterous games and almost counted as a friend, but had gradually drifted away. We knew, of course, that girls were made in a different way from us but she probably found our innocent efforts to extend this knowledge uncongenial. And now she was here, of a sudden, brazenly taller than me, all of nine years old, perhaps even ten, quite grown up.

I have no idea how it came about – some strange conspiracy of hearts perhaps – but we dawdled that whole morning away wandering among the frozen raspberry canes, locked in earnest literary debate. Difficult to discuss the rival merits of Mrs Blyton and Mr Ransome, since I had not read one and she had not read the other, but we did our best and revelled in the effort, finding common ground at last in shared enthusiasm for the hilarious exploits of William Brown. By then, a little drunk with words, I had found myself confessing more than I had ever revealed to a living soul, not even to Mother, awkwardly acknowledging to this sister I never had, how fiction had populated my infant world. Indeed, populated it with more congenial friends than reality ever managed. A solitary child who rarely traded more than a dozen words with anyone, not even his brothers, suddenly enchanted by his first encounter with a girl.

William Brown was much concerned with the opposite sex, his exploits invariably frustrating his older brother's passionate exchanges with a succession of different girls. My new friend amid the raspberry canes now explained how true to life these narratives were. She, too, had a much older brother and could readily confirm that the truth was at least as bad as anything to be found in *Just William*. We had taken literary analysis as far as the second gate of the pub and stood for a while in the gloomy shade of what once must have been an ancient *porte-cochère*, its cobbles strewn with gently steaming clumps of horse manure. She came closer for her denouement, a breathless account of how she once had caught her brother kissing a girl. *He stopped when he saw me, but he was kissing her and I saw.* I remember two woollen mittens taking my arm at this point as she leaned a little closer. *I can show you if you like.* If it was a question, I had no time to reply because she had softly placed her lips on mine, resting them there, her eyes theatrically closed. *Like that,* she said, and sped away into the snows of Toll End Road.

*

I arrived at her kitchen door as she explained about the boiler, and was eventually invited inside. Reluctantly, because I realised her mother had read something in the flushed excitement of her daughter's face and disapproved of my being there. Firing a sidelong glance that left my cheeks burning, I was told to take my shoes off and sit where I was until Mother came to take me home next door. Then, drawing the mittens off and placing a motherly arm around my friend, she led her into an adjoining room, firmly closing the door behind them. She did not look back. Almost at once the muffled sound of a piano appeared, the same scale repeated painfully over and over again, a mournful accompaniment to my reflections on that dreadful kiss, a primal event that comes, even now, flavoured with the scent of hot horses and fear.

So far as I could judge, this next-door house comprised a kind of mirror image of my own, although more luxuriously furnished. I had glimpsed a patterned carpet in the pianist's room and even in the kitchen a strip of rug was laid out on the lino floor. There were cupboards grandly disposed along a wall where our yellow dresser stood. In the middle of the room a polished wooden table was decked out with little vases of flowers and useless things to show that it was not used for eating.

*

I was staring in the direction of the piano scales, calculating that she must have been in a mirror image of our living room, when the door opened and a man came in. He was carrying a little wooden box. Taking pity on my stockinged feet he came across to where I was sitting and said he had brought me something to look at. Apparently, it had once belonged to the much older brother – the one given to kissing – but he had no further use for it. This stranger bearing mysterious gifts was surely Mr Furnivall, although I'd never been this close to him before. In the war, I had sometimes heard him rap at our kitchen door to fetch Father and they would both set off into the war to fight fires. I took his box, holding it stiffly a little above my knees, as proof I did not possess it yet, wondering what it was, wondering more urgently how much he might know about raspberry canes. A confused kind of mirror logic had already led me to conclude that my new friend might share secrets with him the way I shared them with Mother. But he seemed innocent of shameful secrets, simply

42

bending down to free the catch on the front of the box and swing it open, releasing a sharp metallic smell into the air. There was an inner lid recessed in the box, set out with a row of small brass pillars and two black knobs, each with tiny connectors spanning curved arcs of metal studs. An earpiece, or, more exactly, half a pair of headphones, had been poked into a compartment at the side of the box. He said it was a crystal set, a kind of wireless, and that I could keep it if I liked. If I worked at it I could get it going. The earpiece didn't work but there was a shop in Wednesbury that sold things left over from the war and I could get one there. I should tell the man it was for a crystal set and he would know the kind I needed. He might even give me one because nobody wanted them any more.

I spent the rest of that morning sitting alongside him at the polished table while he patiently inducted me into a magical world where sounds could be plucked from thin air with nothing more than a few wires and a piece of crystal. I had no idea why he had chosen me as guardian of these secrets. Much of what he said was lost above my head. Even the simple diagram he drew on a slip of paper was complicated beyond all thought, but I bore the paper home with Mother, clutching the magic box to my chest. She gave me a shilling towards the 1/6d demanded for a pair of headphones that came still wrapped in brown waxed army paper. It was not enough - no sounds emerged from my crystal set, despite its entrancing name. But that is hardly the point in this chronicle - if anyone determined the fatal indecision that characterised my future in two worlds, it was benevolent Mr Furnivall and his passion for wireless. An extraordinary man, whose grasp of electronics easily outstripped many who laid claim to degrees, no one had taught him anything. Undaunted, he had set himself to understand simply for the romance of doing so. This obscure Jude of Ocker Hill in his cramped attic workshop had no interest in university courses. He had taught himself from first principles, with nothing more to hand than library books and a will to understand, and could imagine no other way to learn. He must have been quite exceptionally intelligent - how else would you describe someone who had never bought meters, oscilloscopes, generators or counters - indeed, all the things needed for his work, preferring to make his own? This ability to translate abstractions into concrete physical forms was something close to sorcery and, knowing him, an incorrigibly romantic child who had spent more than half his life in fairyland, paradoxically gravitated to the science stream in school, thinking it a high endeavour. I was wrong.

*

As Mother had knocked the door to fetch me home Mr Furnivall said he had a message for Father. I was to tell him that Mr Harrison knew people at the new Power Station. As he pressed me to confirm that I would not forget what he'd said, I recall my heart lifting with the thought that our all-powerful pirate landlord had somehow found a way to halt the monstrous concrete cooling towers springing up in the village. Taller than the sky and blocking the sun they were blighting our days. One was already blighting the weekly wash, Mother complaining the endless smuts were driving her to despair. I was to tell Father he should go there and like Ali Baba mention the magic word of *Harrison*. It seemed little enough, but was something I was sure he would never do, whatever the prize; so I gave the message to Mother, leaving her to find a way to avoid the hated name. Father must have swallowed his pride. Surely for the only time in his life, he profited from one of those tiny acts of nepotism that had become so much a part of *starting again* in our new world. He worked at the coal-fired power station of Ocker Hill for the rest of his life.

Mr Furnivall had another message. Did I not know there was a picture show in the village most weeks? Other boys like me enjoyed it. I would be very welcome if I wanted to go. Until I was twelve it was free and even after then he was sure my pocket money would run to it. It was a proper picture show, quite like the pictures, held in the Chapel Hall. I should tell Mother that, but she had nothing to worry about, it was a very friendly place and I would come to no harm. Baiting his innocent Methodist hook with Alfred Hitchcock, Mr Furnivall was not to know of the Anglican world awaiting me in Stourbridge. One picture was enough: strange that *The Lady Vanishes*, which filled my dreams for weeks, had left me uneasily to face the ancient choice between the worlds of Saint Mark and Saint Paul. And knowing I could choose neither, hoping to settle for both.

You hardly need theology to mark the contrasting ways of Ocker Hill and Stourbridge: it was written in the very stone. The houses of Ocker Hill were mostly terraced, opening directly onto the pavement with tiny gardens at their rear. There was little green to soften the hard edge of life. Trees were defined as a threat to the crumbling Victorian drains, giving the streets a barren urban air they once had not deserved. Gardens that had fed the war-time inhabitants were not returned to flowers with the coming of peace, but left abandoned in a curious arrested state, awaiting some better world. For those seduced by the modernist dream of *starting again*, the fact that Ocker Hill had escaped war-time demolition unscathed was seen as no more than an accident of history, almost a fault. Civic architects thought those who delighted in the Dickensian charm of insalubrious alleyways were simply victims of their own indulgent nostalgia. If the Germans couldn't bring themselves to demolish Ocker Hill we had the power to do it ourselves. So we did. Without their having much of a say in the matter, the forces of Modernist abstraction bore down on the people of Ocker Hill in the uncompromising reality of concrete and steel. The hope was our eyes would discover a right way of looking at these things, that we would learn to love what was left of our home. We never did.

And Stourbridge? Stourbridge was not like that: its very name forbade it. The houses of Stourbridge, built in centuries that exempted them from demolition, sat placidly on peaceful tree-lined streets. Away from the genteel bustle of its heart were houses with garages for cars and domestic staff to drive them. Houses with gardens that war had barely touched were still bright with flowers. No one strived to reconstruct Stourbridge, the assumption being that it did well enough as it was. No one waited for the wrecking ball to bring a better life.

I got the crystal set to work kneeling in a muddy field one Saturday after school, by then well into my Stourbridge days. The aerial was a fence with wire the necessary lucky length. I had driven my earth into the ground and lay slumped on my side, suffused with that peculiar warmth that comes with impossible things achieved, to hear the first crystal voice. Mindless of the drizzle, I listened to commentary on the annual Boat Race. Cambridge won, although I had no better reason to be partial than the fact The Pot was famously a Cambridge man. He greeted us each morning with the Collect for the Day, little suspecting he had a secret heathen in his midst.

Chapter 6

The first year at Stourbridge was conducted in the Dame School style by two severe yet motherly women. We had a separate red-brick building all to ourselves cut off from the main school by a gated wall. Beyond the boundary of this little school-within-a-school lay a world of men: huge lumpy boys in their hundreds, many in the khaki uniform of the cadet corps, milling about a vast asphalt playground. There would be neither girl as pupil nor woman as teacher in this new world.

My own particular Dame had pinned a paper banner over her blackboard declaring in bright red capitals, LABOR OMNIA VINCIT on the plausible assumption we had not yet met Virgil (and, indeed, that most of us would never meet him). It was years before my brother Ian, schooled in The Pot's sacred Masonic cult of Latin, Greek and Ancient History, told me she had left off a final word - IMPROBUS. Too difficult to translate, she surely meant it as a secret jibe aimed at the irredeemably masculine world awaiting us, revealing, had we the wit to see, that it was all a false pretence. I was yet to learn what many never learn - that it is not *work* which secures the prize in this wicked world, nor even *hard work*, but something altogether less virtuous.

He was in a hurry, our new-broom Headmaster, and expected us to hurry with him. Without further thought he had decided to take the better half of each of the two first-year classes, counted into being as *alpha* and *beta* by Mr Carter on my fateful initial day, and form them into an accelerated class. So far accelerated that they would skip the third year altogether and hurry directly into the fourth. Apparently drawn from the same well of idiocy that so disastrously failed to end the sandwich era, he seemed equally unaware of the misery he would engender in its wake. I recall it puzzled me even then that a little boy could understand what seemed to have escaped a Cambridge brain - that defining half your pupils as inadequate when they had barely left their Dames behind was cruel and ill-conceived. Learning I was destined to be an accelerated boy I wondered whether he realised the crack-pot scheme would land me in my fourth year at the grand old age of twelve, cursed yet again by my birthday?

The truth is I had more potent grounds for regret. After many a lonely week in this bewildering new school I had finally managed to forge a faltering kind of friendship. Most mornings a curious boy, certainly the model for William Brown himself, boarded our morning bus at Princes End, a settlement half-way to Dudley. A tiny chap, tousle-haired, and not always completely dressed, he commandeered the back seat of the bus as a kind of *table de toilette* to arrange himself. We were in the same class, and although my classwork was always beyond reproach, his was almost comically negligent. Homework occupied me for at least an hour each evening in the chilly front room of Leabrook Road, with a pause only when the sound of *The Devil's Gallop* drew me to the kitchen to confirm that Dick Barton had again found the means to survive. My new friend had better things to do with his evening hours. Homework for him, was a dispensable imposition. Such few things he deigned to present for evaluation had been shamelessly copied on the bus, or written to the dictation of one or another randomly recruited schoolgirl en route to Dudley High, truncated mid-sentence by the urgent need to get off. His ability to charm these golden beings left me in awe, but our Dame was less easily seduced. She watched, implacable and unmoved, as he strayed from the path of virtue, slipping inexorably down the order of the class. The removal of *improbus* had been no accident. He would not be joining my accelerated elite, and the injustice of our inevitable separation at The Pot's cruel hand was to hang like a cloud over all that year.

*

On one Wednesday afternoon, seated side by side on the bus, my put-upon friend suggested I break the journey home and visit his house, which turned out to be a pub a short walk down a side street in Princes End. Apparently, I was expected, because his mother had set sandwiches out for us on a table in the public bar, closed until "opening time". We sat together to eat in a comfortable haze of old tobacco smoke and beer, rather like the men of the *Railway Tavern*, talking of this and that. It was when he came to his girlfriend, airily offering to get me one as well, that I became uneasily aware that Mother might not approve of my being here. Remembering raspberry canes, I muttered something incoherent, but he merely leaned back, stretching his tiny legs in a worldly way, and smilingly said *suit yourself*.

A whispered discussion in another room brought his mother back with the key to disarm the bagatelle table that otherwise demanded shillings to deposit the balls. She took the opportunity to size me up and seemed content her boy had secured a friend with tidy hair, congratulating me for producing such a careful knot in my tie. She said she was pleased he was going to Stourbridge and asked whether he helped me with my work as much as he helped the others. The noise of the bagatelle balls rattling down spared me the obligation to reply.

I am sure it was not intended, at least, not at first, but here began my secret life. It was a rare Wednesday now when we would not leave the bus together at Princes End and make our way to the pub. My new best friend was vastly more skilled than me, but the odd freak victory at bagatelle was more than enough to keep me engaged. Besides, there were other pleasures. One week, finding the cupboard beneath the bar unlocked, we washed our sandwiches down with lemonade and beer, ingeniously replacing the empty bottle at the back of the shelf. Aware that Stourbridge determined I must live in separate worlds, I began a kind of double life, hiding one of these worlds from the other. Perhaps this is how spies are made, innocent deceptions shading imperceptibly into bolder lies. One Wednesday, towards the end of the year, the bus conductor at Princes End precipitated the first of these. Rejoining the bus, he had made me pay for the final leg of the broken journey and I remember Mother finding the penny ticket inevitably forgotten in my coat. She heard my mumbled lie and put the ticket on the mantle shelf as her reply. I knew Father would surely press to know more, but when I looked a little later it had gone.

The lure of the secret pub was far more than delinquent bagatelle and beer. He was rich, my friend, with a pound a week to spend, or possibly even more. My own rather unreliable pocket money was a sixpenny coin, but often nothing at all if Mother thought some brother's need was more urgent. This boy had only to ask for fabulous things, his bedroom a pirate's hoard of abandoned toys, cricket bats, air rifles, wireless sets and board games yet to be played.

Of course, it could not last. It was Father who ended the dream, telling me one Tuesday evening that someone had seen me in Princes End. He asked what on earth was I doing in Princes End, forestalling my reply by saying Mother would not have me hanging about a public house. Could I not see that Mother was unhappy I was never at home? And then the hammer fell: henceforth, Wednesday afternoons would be spent in Ocker Hill. The tragic news that I could not come was conveyed on the bus the following day and greeted with a shrug. Disheartened that he was so easily reconciled, I tried again, adding that Father might change his mind, but he grinned and said the game would be up next year in any case. He was wiser than his years, that boy, and knew that schools are tribal places - friendships across classes can never endure. I watched him from the top of my bus that final day, thinking of the friendship of Patroclus and Achilles, a favourite story of our Dame. Walking to the familiar corner, the insouciant satchel at his back as empty as it ever was.

*

Ocker Hill had yet to learn the news, but that first year at my Stourbridge school marked Mother's final year at hers. Mother was a natural teacher, albeit inclined to think too well of those who were not natural pupils. She tempered habitual indulgence with occasional flights of fiery anger when one or another of her angels burnt its wings. She passed her professional life in charge of a reception class and devoted her life to teaching her hoards of unwilling charges to read. The method she adopted for this thankless task involved sing-song repetitions of letter sounds gradually recruited to the service of a growing vocabulary of words. It was a regime of her own invention, peculiar to the point of eccentricity, but successful nonetheless. Astonished parents, long resistant to schooling of any kind and asking little of life, were saddled suddenly with children demanding something to read. Years later, adults remembering with advantage Mrs Kennedy's *call-it* rule, would linger under the classroom window, sometimes even joining in, as forty voices solemnly recited the sounds of the letters w – a – l - k on her board, pausing dramatically for breath, to chorus in triumph, *call it walk*. Long-winded and in many ways absurd, when all else fails, love often finds a way.

Father told us she was leaving the school because she was poorly and needed time to rest. The doctor had put him in charge of her medicine and he gave her a spoonful every evening. The seizures seemed to stop but as Mother sank into lethargy and despair, he must soon enough have realised this was hardly his wished-for cure. Phenobarbital was a word we came to fear. For Mother was no better and the doctor came again.

And what of this doctor, arriving in his little car, bringing the smell of ether with him as he bustled into the house? Father hung on his every word, mumbling hopeful fragments of things the doctor said like charms that might yet work a kind of magic. What would it have helped to know this doctor was no more schooled in science than a child? His medical knowledge of epilepsy, such as it was, had been gleaned long ago from books where epilepsy was no disease at all. Rather, it was a kind of sacred curse, caused by an excess of food or sex. He surely believed it was an affliction of women, peculiarly women. This doctor's books had spoken of quite recent times when colonies of epileptics were best kept apart and not permitted to breed. Gradually, we three boys came to see his kindness as he had secretly defined it for himself: benevolent condescension extended to the paradoxically clever children of the insane. It was then he must have realised it is unwise to dissemble to clever children, paradoxical or not, for they will surely find you out. Whatever the cause, his frequent visits stopped. Suddenly, it seemed more sensible that Mother should visit him. We were no longer witness to the magic words but must hear them at second hand when Father brought them home with Mother. How could I have known then what now I know, that the man was a dangerous fool, his expertise built on craven compliance to antique texts. That his beliefs were as primitive as those of the witches of Wednesbury market and infinitely less safe. Mother's seizures did not improve at his hand, in fact, her injured mind grew worse. The phenobarbital he so glibly prescribed, no doubt attracted to the name, disguised her seizures while tipping them into something far worse. He created the very disorder his remedy could have never cured. Worse even than that, he added more. *Melancholia*, Father said, proud of possessing a name for Mother's distress. He may not know its cause, but at least with a name he had something to confront. He was not to know he administered the cause each evening in Mother's little spoon.

I have only one fugitive clue as to what she herself thought, staring into the pit of depression this careless remedy had opened at her feet. I remember the two of them returning late one night. They had been to see the film *Notorious* at the pictures in Dudley and returned to find us not in bed, albeit Stuart had been left in charge. When neither of them commented, we realised they had barely noticed our mutiny. It was a time they had begun to argue again, to argue more and more, and that was why they were late. When Mother came to hug me, I protested and tried to turn away, but she kept me there and I knew she realised I believed myself too old to see that she had been crying. Strangely, they wanted us to stay up that night, although it was very late. We watched Father miserably pour her nightly dose into the little spoon. Swallowing it, she looked at him and mumbled, *do I have to*? I have wondered since about that film, wondered at its strangely improbable end, Cary Grant finally willing the poisoned Ingrid Bergman to make one final barely conscious bid for escape, wondered whether Mother imagined, for a while at least, that someone might come to take her home.

*

Presents that Christmas, before the time of bicycles, were three unwrapped piles on the dining room table. Some had clearly been hoarded for months, the metal lids of painting sets already showing signs of their storage, but we made the best of what we got, with disputed trades the only source of strife. There was little evidence Father played much part in the selection of presents. He seemed content that it was Mother we thanked. Mother's innocent belief that Ian collected lead soldiers delivered me a box of additional troops

52

each year. She was never to discover I purchased them from him as ore, at an escalating rate as his powers of negotiation flowered. She was equally unaware of my secret furnace behind the chicken shed where I melted them in a tin lid, each satisfying circular ingot emblazoned *Cadbury*.

Mother was determined to make the most of her last Christmas at school, asking Father to find a way to make copies of a tiny image of Santa Claus she had cut from a book. They were to be big enough to cover a wall. It took an hour or more closeted with Mr Furnivall next door for him to find a solution, but he returned with an articulated metal pantagraph, temporarily folded on itself like an accordion. He managed this improbable device under Mother's command, passing her completed pictures to colour in, the five of us working well beyond Ian's time for bed, oblivious of time, me thinking all the time of those happy secret days when Mother had painted the puppet heads.

Those were the years of Arthur Ransome, three green books alongside each Christmas pile. All we waited for, in truth, was Father's annual pilgrimage to the chilly front room armed with a shovel of blazing coals. Thereafter, to be left alone with the doings of Susan, Titty, Roger and John. The year of Mother's pantagraph, thinking he was too old for Ransome, Stuart used her discarded paints to colour the illustrations of his Christmas copy of *Pigeon Post*. I was not too old, and he passed the book to me.

*

The turn of that year brought another, more immediate, change. For reasons I never understood, the morning bus was now joined at Dudley by ten or more boys in Stourbridge livery. A little older than me, I had never seen them before, they swarmed into the empty seats surrounding mine. Too shy to do more than listen, an apparently endless flow of dazzling repartee filled my mornings. I sat in mute adoration as these boys, brilliant beyond my comprehension, seemed tireless, filling the air with golden words. It happened a few days later. Craning round from the seat in front, two boys were in full flow, the challenge of the day to list animals that seemed to have no point. Animals having been exhausted at pangolins, they turned to blobfish, ticks and lice. A momentary silence was extended by an unexpected voice. It seemed someone else was speaking but the voice was certainly mine. My heart pounding, I heard myself say, *Mr Gibb strikes me as having very little point.* There was a gale of laughter and someone pleasantly prodded me from behind. *Old carpentry Gibby? Yes, you're right.*

Chapter 7

A shy little fair-haired boy, prone to blush when girls were teased, was an odd recruit to the boisterous crowd of boys on the morning bus, but I had my uses; in particular, the fact I was a little prudish made me a useful foil in many an early courtship move. At first, I contributed little to the ceaseless tide of comedy, but I soon discovered how little it took to keep my new friends amused and in a few magical days I emerged from a friendless chrysalis state to find myself, if not quite a butterfly, at least a passable moth. My apotheosis came one solemn rain-soaked morning, the bus wet, silent and miserable. A boy at my side, someone I barely knew, turned and said *are you going to make us laugh, Kenners?* I had set myself on the way to becoming a kind of itinerant clown.

By the time that year ended and summer holidays began, I had acquired an air of cockiness disagreeable enough for Father to ask one day whether I was seeing that boy from Princes End again. Mother, realising this unwonted sheen of confidence was barely skin deep, simply asked me stand in the light while she held a pair of Stuart's trousers against my legs. I had returned from my Dame's class, bearing a letter releasing me, *at my parents' discretion*, from short trousers. The letter was duplicated, but Mother took the injunction that boys should return in clothes that were *clean, if ragged*, as a personal slight. If God himself had to find the money, her returning accelerated boy would be clad in new long trousers.

The deed was achieved the following week in a carpeted shop in Stourbridge, where I was obsequiously addressed as *the young gentleman* in hushed third-person exchanges with Mother. That was as far as God would go. Stuart's faded jacket would have to complete my tailoring for the new school year as a hand-me-down, but not before it had been subjected to a mysterious cleansing process that left it smelling powerfully of paraffin, the proud golden parts of its woven badge tinted an unaccustomed green.

That was the year schooling proper began, my days now filled with a bewildering procession of men in gowns. I had feared the intensity of work in this accelerated class, imagining things at double speed but in fact it was the reverse. Left to sink or swim by our own devices, The Pot believed the best would surely survive. Accordingly, he decreed that more than half our time would be set aside to work in supervised seclusion on the exercises of the day. I was too young to prosper in such a regime, and took again to passing unhappy days in fictional worlds. Although not a resident of Stourbridge I had been placed in the School House and my green lapel button proved enough to secure me a borrowing ticket to the Town Library. Thereafter, time that should have been devoted to such novelties as history, geography or mathematics, was spent in lonely isolation devouring Chesterton's tales of Father Brown, the gothic fantasies of Lord Dunsany, the fruits of Richmal Crompton's inexhaustible imagination, and – repeatedly, for he seemed to write so little – my copy of *Pigeon Post*, its illustrations even now warped with Stuart's paint. Had I not one fateful Sunday complained of a nail in my shoe, The Pot's optimistic attachment to intellectual Darwinism would have seen me off for good.

*

Father's dispute with the organist at St Mark's made shoes a pressing concern at home. Ocker Hill had but one cobbler and once Father had determined Mr Bannister was never to mend our shoes, he was left to do the job himself. I often watched him, equipped with a sprouting mouthful of tacks, replacing the worn-out soles of battered relics with suitable approximations fashioned from huge panels of leather hung in his shed. Occasional errors were disguised, as far as possible, with copious quantities of melted blacking run along the sides. It was in the nature of the variety of leather Father used that the undersides of our new shoes took on a slightly convex form, demanding care when walking, but the inconvenience soon passed.

On that particular Sunday, as we were setting out to church, Father examined the nail in my shoe and said I would have to stay behind while he fixed it, it would not take long. But the task was unfinished when they returned, harassed bits of dismembered shoe lying scattered across his bench. He explained I could not go to school in those shoes the following day; Mr Bannister may have time to play the organ but others were not so lucky. Stuart had preserved a second pair of ancient shoes that might be called into service. Dusty, scuffed and battered from long years at school, Mother searched them out, but they were far too small. She went upstairs, returning with a pair of shoes, still in their box. Brand new, she declared the colour good enough: dark blue could pass for black. To my dismay, they fitted well enough and I was despatched to school the following day in Mother's best suede shoes, their dainty pom-pom laces threaded through holes decorated with tiny flowers.

The journey that day was a nightmare. No sooner outside, but it seemed I had equipped myself with clown's clogs at least ten times too large. My face on fire in the bus queue, there was nothing else for others to look at but my feet. It seemed even strangers glanced down and smilingly looked away. Long trousers were a help, of course, but pulled down to cover the worst of the indignity, it became almost impossible to walk.

I sat alone on my wall that morning, legs tucked well out of sight, awaiting the Assembly bell, planning how best I might survive the day, miserably aware I never would. The second half of the morning was designated free study and I might, with luck, secure a secluded desk large enough to conceal my disgrace. But first I had French, and sharp-eyed Major Delaunay, to endure. Several weeks of instruction in French had left me in baffled despair. Major Delaunay revealed himself a convert to The Pot's regime in his very first class, handing round copies of a Simenon novel (one each) and the French-English volume of a dictionary (shared one between two). He then installed himself on the teacher's dais with a different novel of his own and told us to *get on with it*. I had already concluded that the task was impossible, since few of the words on the page were actually in the dictionary provided, but that was of less concern than the need to hide my feet. That, too, proved impossible and soon enough a voice from somewhere behind me broke the calm of scholarship.

Sir, Kennedy's wearing girl's shoes. Can he do that, sir?

For the next hour, giggling variations on this theme punctuated the silence from random locations around the room, all pointedly ignored from the dais. When the bell finally unleashed a chorus of scraping chairs, boys filing out paused to ruffle my hair and prod me as they passed the desk where I sat rooted in my place. The corridor outside filled with passable imitations of girls in various stages of torment. I was left alone with Major Delaunay.

What's this about shoes, Kennedy?

He didn't sound greatly concerned.

A *mistake, sir. My mother was in a rush. I have a long way to come, sir. I would have missed the bus.*

It was a cowardly lie, born of panic, barely worth the telling, but he simply smiled down at me, lifting the lid of his desk to drop the paperback book inside. I had seen that smile before: for a moment, it was certain he knew more than anyone about my mother's shoes.

But you caught the bus?

I nodded.

There's something I wanted to ask, Kennedy. Did you bring your letter back? I don't seem to have it here.

But my uncomprehending look was answer enough. I had given Mother his letter and she had read it but said nothing about taking it back. Opening his mouth, he allowed a single quiet *Ah* to escape, then waved me away.

*

There were two boys waiting outside, apparently deep in conversation. The taller one, known as *Basher*, (a consequence of the inoffensive name, *Bashforth*), said they were going into the town and did I want to come. *To the library*, the other one said, lowering his voice, adding, *to consult the Book of the Dead.* It struck me even then that The Pot might disapprove of boys wandering abroad in the town, but I was too far gone in misery for legal quibbles and hobbled after them through the open gates, hands pressed deep into unaccustomed pockets to cover the worst, content that our period of free time would run into the mid-day break. I might at least secure a few more precious hours of relief.

We spent that lunchtime poring over the stages of mummification set out in the *Egyptian Book of the Dead*, a massive leather-bound double folio dragged from a bottom shelf. The work of the morning - translating the three set pages of *Les Demoiselles de Concarneau* - seemed no less ghoulish. To my boundless relief, no mention at all was made of shoes. I was far too timid to relish our state of blatant truancy and puzzled these two boys had thought it worth the risk for no greater reward than an hour in the town library. *Why*, I asked myself, draw me into their futile gesture? It was when the library clock eventually signalled the school's official lunchtime break and they proposed we sit on the municipal benches outside to eat our sandwiches, that I got my answer and finally understood what these two boys were about. For reasons too obscure to explore they had placed me under their protection, taking pity on my plight, shoes and all. I walked back to the school with them, joining the boys coming legally back, torn between relief and humiliation, lost in a confused fever of calculation.

*

I was late getting home that dreadful day, having deliberately hobbled my way to the bus station to avoid the torment of the habitual bus. Mother was sitting in her chair in the kitchen. Ian and Father were peering over her shoulder at Major Delaunay's letter which lay face-down in her lap. She watched me take the shoes off and drop them under the table where stood the empty box that had waited there all day. Ian went to pick them up but Father shouted to leave them alone for God's sake and go and get my own from the shed; and he didn't want to hear another word about bloody shoes. Mother swung round and grabbed his arm. *Don't Bob, not with the children. I'm sorry, love, I'm really sorry.* I knew this last was meant for me and I could see she had been crying again, her eyes ringed a painful red. But saying sorry had made it worse, confirming she must have known all the time and still let me suffer. I pulled away when she went to hold me. No one would ever hold me again, that much was sure. Not after today. I padded upstairs in stockinged feet to sit in my bedroom staring at the patch of rosebay willowherb across the street where I would play never again. Staring sightlessly into a dark future, certain of one thing only: never again would I set foot in that hellish school.

The familiar smell of shepherd's pie crept up the stairs and I remembered I was hungry, but nobody came to fetch me. I heard Stuart go downstairs for his tea. He spent more and more time in his bedroom now, doing homework. I heard them talking and wondered how much he had told them about my clown shoes. He must surely have known, because the whole school seemed to know. Ian came upstairs to look at me, standing swinging on the door, saying I would miss Dick Barton and Mother wanted to know what to do with my tea because she wasn't bringing it up here. I told him to eat it himself, knowing Mother was sure to come up after that. But no one came for a long time, until it seemed the room was becoming quite dark; and then it was Father. And he had the letter in his hand.

It was Major Delaunay's letter, but had been The Pot's idea to broaden our horizons with a trip to France. We would learn to spread our wings in wider landscapes; hear voices in another tongue; see how other children fared in other schools; discover different ways of seeing the world. He told us how lucky we were to live for a while in a famous school near Paris. The Lycée Lakanal had produced generations of authors, artists, scientists, and politicians. This was to be the glamorous destination for the first of many pilgrimages his King Edward's boys would make.

It was decided that all the accelerated boys would go, although my own progress in French could hardly have been a deciding factor. The letter now in Father's hands asked for parental consent. Irresistibly unsealed, I had read it on the bus. The excursion *en masse*, it said, would cost next to nothing, the only additional expense being boys' pocket cash. Well-meaning Major Delaunay! Unaware in all his ingenuous plans of the yawning chasm that lay between his world and ours, the world of Ocker Hill. Fatally unaware that even *next to nothing* was far too much when *nothing* was all you had.

The cost of the excursion had been spelled out in words rather than numbers, a formality giving additional weight to a sum inconceivably beyond what anyone might pay for so small thing as a holiday, even a holiday to France. There was a reminder that parents should ensure no boy brought with him more than *fifteen pounds in bank notes*. That would avoid the sum involved being set against their annual overseas currency allowance. It is difficult to imagine he had considered the stunned awe with which these words were greeted in Leabrook Road, where the occupants had never had cause to consider their annual overseas currency allowance. My pocket money in the best of weeks was a sixpenny coin. There are forty sixpences in a pound. To amass my fifteen pounds would take eleven years. It was unlikely that Major Delaunay would wait that long.

Father dropped the letter on the bed at my side: *I've signed your letter, mind you hand it in tomorrow. Your Aunt Bessie says she'll pay for you to go. She thinks it'll do you good. Now go and thank your mother for asking. She's got enough to worry about without having you sulking up here. And I don't want to hear another word about shoes.*

Chapter 8

He was right, of course. Those few dreadful days had had nothing to do with footwear, nothing at all. Mother's gesture that morning sending me to school in girls' shoes had been yet one more round in the battle with Father over the kind of life each of them wanted for me. Battles in a war both were bound to lose. For Father, a trip abroad had the smack of Scouting about it, with the prospect of curing my irrational fear of the dormitory. Just what was needed to snip an apron string or two and ready me for the bracing truths of life. And Mother? Poor Mother: what better symbol of her hopeless state than those remnants of broken shoes? That they were my shoes in particular, and that Father had not completed the job, surely played its part. Illness and the aftermath of war had conspired to spring a trap all three of her sisters had escaped: Alice and Mary now in far-off comfortable Canada; Bessie to a life of unimaginable luxury with a prosperous husband in leafy Solihull. It is too late now and too far off; I can only guess at what she imagined those pom-pom shoes might yet have achieved. Perhaps she felt my humiliation a price worth paying for both of us if it meant I must stay behind. She would at least hold on to the daughter she never had; keep me close. Born of phenobarbital, it was the first truly mad act I saw her commit. It would not be the last. It also made my going to France virtually certain. Once it became a matter of principle for Father, his pride determined the outcome, whatever the cost. Although how, exactly, he persuaded Mother to plead with her sister for the money, and the price he paid for that somewhat grudging endowment, is a topic to which we shall return.

I left Leabrook Road a few weeks later feeling brand-new and richer than I had ever been. Mother had disguised the battered ten-shilling note that had lived out its war inside a biscuit barrel, folding it into a brand-new pound note. Both now were inside my brand-new passport, all these riches to be handed for safe keeping to Major

Delaunay. Before boarding the bus in the school playground, Stuart had handed me his shiny new half-crown, saying *bring it back, it's for the telescope*. It was a private joke - he knew I sometimes cast him as Captain John in the story of the Swallows and the Amazons. But if he meant my fictional friends would be keeping him company while I was away, it was an assurance sought in vain – I was certainly taking them with me.

*

Much to my surprise, I quite enjoyed the novelty of French dormitory life, soon discovering that the boys reluctant to undress were those with sisters at home, an impediment I had avoided. While they were hiding their nakedness with one absurdity or another, some even sitting under the bed to change into pyjamas, life with my brothers had made modesty a luxury not worth preserving. I earned the odd approving glance that first night as I hopped into rough French sheets in my habitual summer naked state. We slept fourteen to a room, our allocated senior boy perched above us in a curious elevated structure a little like a glazed hen-house with its own little door. I had imagined many fearful things on the journey here, but drifted happily to sleep that first night, the cheerful call *lights out, you chaps*, bringing thoughts of Jennings and Darbishire.

We were woken the following morning by a little boy walking through the dormitory with a handbell. Woken to discover the Spartan truth of breakfast at the Lycée Lakanal - a slice of imperfectly toasted bread, milky coffee served in unaccustomed bowls, and thick plum jam tasting of crystallised sugar, prised from rustic jars positioned one between two. We took turns with the single sticky spoon. Major Delaunay stationed himself at the head of our table, rejected his coffee with a frown, lit a cigarette, puffed expansively into the morning air, and told us to present ourselves after breakfast in the Hall where someone from a bank would exchange our money. To avoid leaving it to the last minute, when we would no doubt have nothing left to spend, we were told to walk that very morning into a town not far away. There, we would be able to purchase postcards, stamps and presents for our parents, to be kept in store until the morning of our departure. We could use what funds were left as pocket money. He was sure we would spend the lot before the fortnight was out, but not to come knocking at his door for more if we did.

Thanks to the alchemy of international finance, I strode into the little town of Sceaux later that morning with the assurance of a Rothschild, possessed of a sheaf of banknotes almost too thick to fold into my purse, my only concern how on earth I would find time to spend this wholly unexpected fortune. I had been first in the queue at the door to the Hall waiting for the man from the bank to change my precious notes. He was late to arrive, led in with some ceremony by the little boy who had rung the handbell and a man dressed like a railway porter, carrying a kind of metal suitcase with folding legs that opened to reveal a multitude of little pigeon holes filled with multi-coloured bank notes. The bank man pushed past the boys in the doorway, seated himself at a table, adjusted his glasses, examined his folding suitcase, and rattled off what seemed like a command to Major Delaunay. Getting no reply, he tried again, speaking in a slow elaborate way as to a child. Major Delaunay frowned back at him, shook his head, and called across to Mr Lucy who was holding us back at the doorway, *what's this chap on about, Lucy? I can't make his gabble out.*

I watched this little piece of theatre, suddenly overwhelmed by dark clouds of doubt. How could Major Delaunay possibly not have understood? The little bank man with his tiny beard, the very image of the Professor in *Rupert the Bear*, had certainly been speaking French. And he had not been gabbling at all - in fact, he had been speaking so slowly that anyone who understood French must have understood. And Major Delaunay's mastery of this mysterious tongue had famously brought him unscathed through a terrible war; had helped him bluff his way past prison guards; had allowed him effortlessly to deceive foreign spies. All this was common knowledge. How on earth could he not have understood? Mr Lucy, who seemed to know perfectly well what the bank man had said, let go of my collar and pushed me into the room, telling me to go and collect my money and go out by the other door. He called across to Major

Delaunay, *not now, old man, poke your stick some other time.*

Major Delaunay recognised me as I arrived at the little improvised counter clutching the receipt for my sacred thirty shillings. To my astonishment, he gave me an elaborate wink, smiled into my bewildered face and walked across to the other door, growling to no one in particular, *that sort wasn't giving the orders not so long ago. Pleased enough to see us then. Who the hell did he think he was talking to? Sorry, Lucy old chap, just can't stand the type.*

He was standing in the corridor when I came out and walked with me out into the garden and down to the main gate. *Well, Kennedy, what d'you think of Paris?* I told him we really hadn't seen very much of it, but it seemed very big, very dusty, and a bit smelly. *But all the bomb damage, Kennedy, what about that? You wouldn't call that inconsequential, would you?* I was not entirely sure of the word, but I said Father had told me the Germans hadn't bombed Paris like they had bombed Coventry. *And why's that, d'you think, Kennedy?* I said I didn't know, but Father had said he wouldn't have let me come if there had still been Germans here. He burst out laughing, stopping to perch himself on a stone bench next to a little water fountain and light a cigarette. Since he seemed deep in thought and showed no signs of walking any further with me, I felt constrained to stay where I was, albeit in a fever of impatience to reach the shops before someone else had bought all the best things.

Eventually he noticed I was there and muttered, *we sent them packing, you see. You can tell your father that. Chaps like that fellow in there with the money-bags left it to chaps like me to send the Germans packing. We weren't so inconsequential then.* He was nodding in the direction of the road as if to say he wasn't walking any further and I was sent on my way. Someone told me later that the bank man had complained to Major Delaunay about having to deal with inconsequential English schoolchildren, the remark was so obviously justified, given the pitifully inadequate sum I had innocently presented for exchange, Major Delaunay had taken it on himself to be offended on my behalf. The discussion with Mr Lucy had confirmed the surprising fact that the implicit hierarchy of class among our masters was the equal of anything Ocker Hill could offer. The Major would not, of course, wear a monocle at school or even here, but we had read *The Toff* and believed there were circumstances where he did. In a word, we knew him for the hero our war-blighted years craved. That he made so little effort to disguise the fact he loathed boys indiscriminately, served only to increase our respect. I could see he had taken pity on me, but you did not need long to conclude that Major Delauney disliked the workings of a State that had sought out boys to educate simply because they were clever. It was not enough; and he viewed the passing of his once-ordered world as the greatest betrayal of a war he no longer believed had been won.

*

The only thing on display in the shop window that I was certain Mother would like was a music box in the form of a miniature grand piano. It was meant as a jewel box, albeit a very small one, the lacquered lid opening to reveal a small space that already contained a few unconvincing imitations. The woman in the shop saw that I had set my heart on it and nodded approvingly when I said it was for my mother. She prized the bundle of bank notes from my hand, licked her finger, and began rapidly rifling through them, pausing now and then to sigh very audibly. I had lifted the lid of the tiny piano and was already captivated by the tinkly sound of The *Blue Danube* waltz. She seemed very nice, this motherly French woman who spoke to me in English, but I could not entirely supress the unworthy thought that now she had taken my money she might cheat me. It could not be every day she encountered riches on such a scale. I was wondering how many notes in my bundle I would be left with, when she took the tiny piano from my hand and said something that sounded like *alas* with a shake of the head. *There was not enough, did I see, Cherie? Not quite enough.* It was the first time someone had called me *Cherie*, which made me feel French and slightly grown-up, but it was mortifying to realise the piano was so much more valuable than I had imagined. It seemed unimaginable to be dispossessed at a stroke of all my wealth and I began to feel sorry I had chosen it. She was still holding my bundle of notes and I was put to thinking how I could possibly rescue them. The bank man had taken my only English notes - there were no others. She saw me reach for the purse in my pocket, heavy with copper coins, but shook her head. I knew she was right; I had already bought my postcards on the way here and the old man in the shop had taken almost all the coins proffered on my outstretched palm. Coins didn't take you very far at all in France. I realised she was still talking, shuffling the bundle of bank notes back and forth, the way Mother shuffled cards when we were playing whist. Suddenly, she stuffed the money into her apron, reached under the counter for a box and put my prize inside, pausing only to add a minute bottle, no bigger than a thumbnail, saying *for your Maman.*

I secured a little undeserved esteem among my companions of the bedchamber with my exotic purchase, even letting them hear it play for a few seconds. But in spending all my money I had undeniably broken Major Delaunay's rule, before the holiday had even started. And the consequences were not long coming. My little breakfast gang had discovered it was possible to supplement the inadequate breakfast toast with a kind of hot cheese sandwich available at any number of street cafeterias outside; indeed, they had obviously been set up to meet that very need. Lemonade was preferable to weak coffee and we soon learned enough French to order the addition of grenadine. These things were not at all expensive, but as my meagre store of coins dwindled, I was soon forced to find excuses to stay behind.

Mr Lucy provided the metro tickets for our daily journeys into Paris. Depending on the excursion of the day, vouchers were also handed out to secure admission to the Louvre Museum, the Sainte Chapelle, Notre Dame, Sacré Coeur and apparently numberless other sites pre-selected by The Pot for our improvement. Unfortunately, he had vastly over-estimated our appetite for high culture and under-estimated the appeal of numerous less elevated activities Paris had on offer. It was not long before the senior boys charged with marshalling us along the tunnels between one metro station and the next mysteriously detached themselves, only to reappear at the point of assembly for the return to the school. Faced with the prospect of open revolt, the two masters left in charge had little option but to fall in with substantial revisions to the planned activities. The Pot would certainly have considered an ascent of the Eiffel Tower as less than strictly educational and probably had similar views on boat trips on the Seine, time spent on the suicidally dangerous swings in the public parks of Paris or on afternoons spent in tiny rowing boats not greatly different from those available for hire in Stourbridge. My own reservations were more immediate and more personal: since there were no vouchers for the *Tour Eiffel*, none for the *Bateaux Mouches*, and certainly none for rowing boats, I found myself increasingly in search of excuses to be left behind.

Later in that first week we were left to our own devices for the whole of the morning, on condition that we stayed within the school grounds. I was about to retreat with a book when the boy at my side, having finished his toast and coffee, proposed adjourning to another dormitory where somebody was organising a game of cards. Hours spent with Mother and Stuart playing three-handed whist made the prospect appealing and I trailed after him down the corridor and into the dormitory next to our own. Four or five boys were standing silently alongside one of the beds. The tall boy who slept in the glazed hen-house in our own dormitory was also there, apparently waiting for our arrival. He pushed a bank note into my hand and said I was to treat it as a loan and that I could pay him back with my winnings. It was too late to protest, because he had already snatched the note back and tossed it onto the bed to join a multi-coloured carpet of other notes already there.

There was something unsettling about this peculiar gathering of silent boys, shuffling apart to make room for me. I realised they were waiting for me to pick up the single card lying face down on the bed in front of where I stood. I could see each of the other boys already held a card in his hand. I picked mine up with a sense of rising panic, realising that French cards may well be different. I glanced down at it. A bearded man with a pike on his shoulder, the letter B and a heart. It must be the Jack of hearts, but the name hardly mattered since I could hardly play a game without knowing the rules. I looked across at the boy who had lent me the bank note, thinking it seemed unfair to have to repay a loan I had not even asked for. One by one the boys tossed their cards onto the bed. The tall boy gathered up the bank notes from the bed, extracted one from the pile, pocketed it, and shoved the rest of the money into my hand saying I had won. He didn't suggest another round of the game or even say what the game had been. One of the boys had already gathered up the cards and joined the others as they drifted away.

I walked a little taller in the days that remained, took my turn at the oars in the little boats, perched myself on wicker chairs, gossiping over lemonade and grenadine. Even – although I rather regretted it – persuaded another boy to join me in the empty lift in the Eiffel Tower. No one, it seemed, envied my sudden wealth. Since no one suggested another game of cards, I learned to call myself lucky.

*

The Pot's long-planned Paris excursion came to a dramatic end with the decision to take revenge for the catalogue of indignities and petty humiliations that came to characterise our time in the Lycée Lakanal. It was a decision that emerged in the group without discussion. Without taking conscious thought, we realised how deeply we resented the sullen janitor in a leather apron who had taken it on himself to rule over us once our masters ceased trying. We had arrived at his little fiefdom the confident children of King Edward VI, believing ourselves the equals of any. That was not how this leather-clad martinet saw things. In his eyes we were little better than ill-disciplined ruffians with philistine tastes, a shameful ignorance of the glories of Paris, and a pitiful command of the language. He set out to teach us how little sway we might exert in an altogether superior school. Major Delaunay had helped win the war. Knowing this, it had been painful enough to witness his impotence faced with the word *inconsequential*. Mr Lucy's craven inclination to curry favour with our enemy had been far worse. Since vengeance was demanded, vengeance it would be. We were not sure how, or even when, but were strangely confident that fate would deliver the means.

The boys in the neighbouring dormitory had set their hearts on a pillow fight to take place on our last night. A form of combat unavailable in Stourbridge, pillow fights - along with dormitory feasts and rags (an obscure word of uncertain sense) - featured large in the school stories that filled our days. Children actually slept in

69

the schools where Jennings, Wharton, Bunter, Psmith, and many another, spent their busy days. Public Schools, where Houses were not merely buttons to wear in your lapel, but places where you lived, slept, ate, and had your being. Although they barely mentioned it, even the Swallows went away to school – the boys to one, girls to another - and brought their codes of honour home. Schools, in fact – although we were loathe to admit it – not at all unlike our present superior prison.

The pillows of the Lycée Lakanal turned out to be entirely unsuited to any kind of fight. Since they were little more than linen sacks, crudely stitched shut, the first blow simply produced a shower of dusty feathers. The exchange of two blows was enough to end the fight. Given the peculiar smell of duck down, it would have been impossible to sleep. The event would surely have been abandoned were it not for the arrival of our aproned tormentor in the courtyard below to investigate the noise. By unspoken mutual consent his angry upturned face in the livid electric light became the target of a succession of emptied pillows. Too startled to move, he stood, impotent and thigh-deep in a field of duck feathers as we queued to take turns at the open window. I emptied mine near the half-way mark, the courtyard below already billowing white.

*

We left in disgrace the following morning, following a long and utterly incomprehensible public scolding. Breakfast reluctantly served, we were summoned to the Hall where a man we had never seen before addressed us at inordinate length in French. Quietly agitated he was clearly unused to anger, managing a kind of supressed rage. It is possible he believed we understood what he was saying. Not knowing what we should do when he finished, we innocently burst into rapturous applause, leaving Major Delaunay to call for quiet. As the unknown man bustled away, we were told our punishment: we must use the time we had before the arrival of our bus to sweep the courtyard. There were not enough brooms, and it was soon only too evident that brooms were quite unsuited to the task, but we did the best we could.

I bore my trophy home to Mother, who treasured it for many years. I recall she handed it to me not long before she died, her eyes creased with painful recollection, explaining how Stuart had bought it for her in Paris on a school trip many years ago.

Chapter 9

Father's part in the decision to send me on the school trip to Paris had its roots fifty years before, and in another world altogether. In 1905, Leslie Lancaster, an up-and-coming Birmingham businessman, persuaded his father Martin to build two large interconnected houses on a virgin plot of land in Solihull, a newly established dormitory suburb of the city. The houses were to be built in the Arts and Crafts style then in vogue – a bit like the fictional one Soames Forsyth commissioned from the doomed Phillip Bossiney. It was a substantial investment - in the region of half a million pounds - because Leslie, a keen amateur astronomer, indulged his hobby by building an observatory in the garden. The roof had to be thatched, to preserve the quaint style of the house, but since it also had to rotate, it was a complicated and extremely expensive project.

Leslie Lancaster modestly describes himself as a "printer" in the 1911 census, but by then he and his elder brother Lewis had taken control of their father's business in Birmingham and both derived substantial incomes from a number of patented inventions. These included the familiar blue cartridge-shaped cardboard holders that banks still use to transport coins, but their fortune rested on "the workman's pay packet" - a stiff paper envelope with an ingenious flap allowing bank notes to protrude but not to be withdrawn until a seal was broken. Any cash inside could be counted through small punched holes. The two brothers prospered in Edwardian Birmingham and their elegant houses in Ashleigh Road took on a political significance, becoming part of an informal base for Joseph Chamberlain's new Liberal Unionist Party. By 1913 both were influential City Councillors; in 1928, Lewis became Lord Mayor.

In 1939, the year I was born, Leslie Lancaster got married. It was a love match, but undoubtedly a surprise. The groom was 57 years old and had appeared long reconciled to an agreeable bachelor style of life, dividing his time between the printing presses of Shadwick

Street, exploration of the surface of the moon, and annual motoring holidays on the Côte d'Azur. He had also become a generous patron of the City's bourgeoning Orchestra, founded in 1920 with a spectacular opening season which saw Elgar himself conduct a performance of his cello concerto. It was through these musical connections that Leslie met his bride: Bessie Cowley, twenty years his junior, a spirited women with a commanding presence and rich contralto voice that had secured her a place in the orchestra's Chorus. Bessie was my mother's sister.

I have few memories of my Uncle Leslie who, even then, seemed like someone better suited to the films of David Lean than to my Ocker Hill reality. He was a huge man with a drooping moustache a little like Mr Harrison's but, unlike our benevolent pirate neighbour, invariably clad in a complicated knickerbocker suit of unyielding tweed. The last time I saw him was shortly after my accession to Stourbridge: perhaps the event had been some kind of celebration, because I sensed myself to be in some way the centre of attention. A bear of a man suddenly loomed over me, grasping my hand and leading me through the dark of the garden and into a thatched house smelling of the apples that were stored in drawers ranged along its walls. I had often played in there and knew that the narrow door at the end of the room was invariably kept locked. That night it was thrown open and my uncle pushed me into the dim green light of an octagonal space filled with the throbbing sound of turning gears and the smell of hot mechanical oil. I remember staring up at a patch of star-studded sky through a surprising slot high in the roof and my Auntie Bessie, who had been waiting for us, trying to lift me up to see. She abandoned the effort and told me I was there as a special treat to look at the moon through uncle's telescope. An irritated gravelly voice far above my head shouted that the child should look down not up but I cannot recall seeing anything in either direction, and certainly not the moon.

Later that evening, allowed to stay up as an additional treat, we set up camp under a dinner party table and I watched my cousin Alastair daringly knot his father's shoe-laces together. I played no active part in the business, although I watched with some satisfaction, rather resenting being thought a child. The retribution, delivered later that night as I lay in my foreign bed, was muted, Mother saying I should be ashamed of myself with Uncle Leslie so poorly. I never saw him again.

When Uncle Leslie died, his Solihull household comprised a cook, a chauffeur-gardener, and a "skivvy" – a harassed little girl barely older than me, moving silently from room to room about her duties like some Chekhovian serf. With my cousin away at boarding school, visits to Solihull became more and more frequent. Although the invitation was invariably extended to *Dorothy and the boys* (we could hardly be left behind), that convinced no one: Aunt Bessie's empty tearful house manifestly lacked a man and it was to Father she turned. To Mother's jealous dismay, far from resenting the role, he seemed content to become a kind of hireling, even proud to be managing her sister's house, a house that was not his own. As the months drew into winter, calls on his time grew more frequent and Mother complained that a journey by bus, tram and train was simply too much. That was the week we found ourselves in possession of the Austin "Big Seven" car. The vehicle had been garaged in reserve for the Lancasters since before the war: now it was ours, although we had barely the means to use it. When Mother complained that the phone box in Toll End Road was too far to walk and not always clean, the Kennedy family – incredibly - took possession of the first domestic telephone in Leabrook Road. Settling the bill for a school trip had been a small enough gesture to cement my all-too-willing father in his decidedly ambiguous role.

*

I am on the bus with Mother, not sure where we are going, until we reach the train station and I realise it is to Auntie Bessie's. Mother is wearing the blue coat she only wore to go to church. And a hat with a pin at the side that she keeps pressing to make sure it is still there. She lets me take the train tickets because she knows I like giving them to the man at the gate but she hardly speaks at all. When we reach the top of Ashleigh Road she stands inside the bus shelter and looks at herself in the little mirror in her bag and suddenly says, *come on then, best get it over with*. She walks on ahead almost as if she didn't want a boy in his school uniform at her side.

There are many things I will never know about that dreadful day: why I was not at school; where my brothers were; why Father had seemed not to know where we were going, but had never asked; why I was conscious of an awful sense of impending calamity. Auntie Bessie seemed surprised to see us, asking why the car wasn't there; where was Bob? I remember her saying *did we want to come in* and thinking it a strange thing to ask when we had come so far, but Mother was already hanging her coat up in the hall so it hardly mattered. She walked into the kitchen and I went to follow her, but Auntie Bessie barred the way, pushing me into another room and closing the door.

I was in the room they used to sit in to listen to music on the gramophone. You could hear the music they played here even in the bedroom, huge orchestral sounds swirling about, but I had never been allowed inside. Tall boxes of records were stacked in shelves edge-on. I took one down and sat on the carpet to open it, laying out three glossy black disks in tissue paper, each bearing the label *Schubert Symphony Number 8 (Unfinished)*. The smell of cold shellac rose up to meet me, oddly foreign, unattainably luxurious. The gramophone itself was on the other side of the room - a polished cabinet with fretted sides. I went across and was about to raise the lid when the door to the room swung open and Auntie Bessie shouted that I must *take this viper home*, something breaking in her voice that made my heart jump. Mother was in the hall putting her coat on. She saw me and asked whether I wanted something to drink: *she could fetch me a drink if I wanted one, I had only to say*. I knew she could not have meant what she said about the drink because she had already gone outside and was walking down the path. I went to pick up the records but Auntie Bessie said *leave them where they are, go with your mother*.

*

I spent the journey home, pining for the unexpected kindness of the Lycée Lakanal, dreading the inevitable domestic row. But Father never asked about our visit to Solihull, never mentioning it at all, meekly finding time to stuff our morning satchels with improvised sandwiches, because in the days that followed, more often than not, Mother was still in bed at breakfast time. My dictionary for the new school year had confirmed the definition of *viper* beyond correction and I dared not ask further. Certainly not ask a mother suddenly drained of life, someone I hardly knew, aimlessly sitting in a dressing gown. It was not long before the doctor entered our lives again. Father said her *melancholia* had got much worse. He might have said she was depressed or sad or many other words, but never used another term. I could only feel the word was somehow not big enough, too gently poetic for someone who barely ate, passing her time staring into space. Someone, increasingly, who never spoke, apart from a mumbled ritual resistance to the nightly little spoon.

The treatment ordained for Mother was called electro-convulsive therapy; the place where it was to be administered, a hospital in Wolverhampton. Not that she needed to spend the night. It took no time at all to attach electrodes on her skull and the machine to deliver the pulse of current to her brain was the latest of its kind. The shock produces a massive convulsion, enough to break your limbs, but the paradox of this orchestrated insult to the brain – or so it was claimed - is the patient cannot remember the event at all: the shock erases the record of its own effects. We are eighty years on with this doubtful therapy and still unsure whether this claim is true. But certainly no one now would follow the barbaric reasoning used in Mother's day, that since she would not remember the consequences, the shock could be delivered without anaesthetic. Had I been old enough, I would have known *unmodified ECT* for the hideous witchcraft it surely was. Unable to extract Mother's melancholy, it was to be left in place. Her not knowing it was there would have to suffice. In a word, she would no longer remember to be sad and that was to count as her cure. She endured five sessions of unmodified ECT before she found the means to escape. I was never to know in detail *how* this came about, although I can be exact as to *when*. It was bonfire night.

*

Ian came top of the county of Staffordshire in the eleven-plus examinations, earning himself an illustrated copy of the *Just So Stories* of Rudyard Kipling and the right to decline a place in Tipton's newly prefabricated Grammar School and join his brothers in distant Stourbridge. Those were days the three of us left our silent house each morning with an unstated sense of relief, aware that an altered Mother was still in bed. I made a poor start to my entry into 4S, the unimaginatively named science fourth year, and it was not long before I regretted the folly of committing myself to subjects for which I had neither taste nor aptitude. I retreated into more sophisticated versions of fairyland, better suited to my sudden teenage status and as a quixotic reproach to mathematics began to write poetry, daringly in the style of Dylan Thomas. As I slipped inexorably down the order of the class, I came casually to see myself as my teachers saw me - one more little boy, his early promise burnt out, set fair on a course to nothing.

One evening, calling a truce in a nightly battle with trigonometry, I asked Mother whether I could accept Mr Furnivall's invitation and go to the picture show. I knew it was that night because I had seen him set off, impressively armed with what I took to be reels of film. She said I would be wasting my time and must mind who I talked to, but that I could go on condition I prepared my things for the morning. I arrived at the Methodist Chapel only just in time. Divested of twopence at the door I was left free to sit anywhere in an almost empty room, lit by the silver light of a huge white screen.

That winter night came to define Thursdays as tiny oases in the dreary schoolwork trudge to Christmas in Form 4S. The films selected by Mr Furnivall more than redeemed him for the inadvertent sin of luring me to the cause of science. In a few brief years, in the grubby hall of a Methodist Chapel, I consumed the whole canon of a Golden Age of cinema, becoming familiar in ways my Lycée friends would hardly credit with the works of David Lean, Michael Powell, Basil Dearden, Alfred Hitchcock, Emeric Pressburger, Carol Reed and many another. Television had yet to arrive in Leabrook Road and I came to these giants with completely innocent eyes, sharing, if only for an hour or two, magic lives obscurely suffused with purpose denied to me; entering worlds better than my own. I walked home in the dark that first Thursday night, desperate to share with Mother my exultant state, rehearsing what to say about people it seemed I had always known in some other life that I must somehow have overlooked. Perhaps it was as well that Father said she had gone back to bed, I doubt I could have found the words.

*

Bonfire Night the year I entered Form 4S was blighted by vindictive quadratic equations, set as punishment for indiscipline. There was a formula to apply, and that was easy enough, but since Mr Carter never explained its derivation, let alone its purpose, the fact that there were invariably two solutions to each problem plagued me. I sat, head bowed, at the dining room table, close to tears, frustrated by an activity that seemed arbitrary and perverse. If this indeed was science, truly I had chosen to blight my own life. I must have reached the half-way point, already aware that the more difficult examples were still to come, when the smell of smoke outside became unbearable. Ian, boasting an extra layer of clothing against the cold, came yet again to ask how long I would be. Knowing all too well the cost, I decided to finish the work on the bus tomorrow, closed the book, and went out with him into the night.

Our collection of fireworks had been painfully purchased one by one from scraps of pocket money over the course of several weeks. Hoarded in a precious communal tin they were now in Stuart's charge: two packets of grey sparklers, three small Catherine wheels, two Roman candles and (Father's contribution) a single modest rocket, to be fired from a milk bottle at the close of play. Our principal purchases, however, were the miniature hand-grenades known as *bangers*. We bought as many of these as our innocent smiles could secure, because they were not for the use of children and shopkeepers were becoming increasingly cautious. These stubby cardboard tubes, packed with gunpowder and with a twist of blue touchpaper at one end, came with printed instructions that they were to be lit and either tossed girlishly to the ground or left to explode at a safe distance. The urchins of Ocker Hill put them to better use, treating the fizzing five-second fuse as a challenge and launching them as late as possible to explode in mid-air.

Guy Fawkes may well have played some part in better-mannered places and stuffed effigies were probably placed on the unassuming fires of Stourbridge, but bonfire night in Ocker Hill was fashioned from different metal altogether. Even in my fourth year at school it remained an unpardonably dangerous re-enactment of the war that had passed us by. The present war between the thirty or so houses of Leabrook Road was ferociously good-natured, undeclared, and lasted but a single night. The narrow gardens of each house boasted their own fire, set in honeycomb circles of brick, piled high with discarded doors, offcuts of planking, asphalt roofing, old tyres, tea chests, broken furniture and prodigious quantities of straw illegally dosed with sump oil. It had been the tar-laden smoke from Father's fire, the work of several days, that won the proxy battle with Mr Carter's quadratics.

It was customary to invade neighbouring fires as the mood took us, venturing as far as Toll End Road, but we lingered round our own that night. Remembering his Scouting days, Father had poked baking potatoes between the bricks of the fire and was busy saving them from incineration. Drawn by the smell of cooking, even an enemy or two had arrived to declare a temporary ceasefire. As I began on my charred potato, I was suddenly aware of a figure silhouetted against the lights of the house picking its way down the path towards us. I recognised the man who drove Auntie Bessie's car, the man who would cut a circle of turf from one of the lawns of Ashleigh Road so that we could play putting. He offered Father a cigarette and they stood red-faced against the heat of the fire, talking quietly together. I realised my cousin Alastair was standing awkwardly at the top of the steps, dressed in full school uniform, and apparently unwilling to risk his shoes on the path to the fire. He was holding a white enamel bucket. When the man – I think his name was Mr Jencks – said that he would have to go and look out for the car, it being bonfire night, I realised Aunt Bessie must have come. Even now she could be with Mother in the house. My head filled with *vipers*, I followed Mr Jencks up the path to where Alastair stood. Father stayed behind, loftily unconcerned, tending his fire. Alastair silently held the bucket out to Stuart. It was filled with fireworks – more than we could have collected in a lifetime.

For the rest of that night, Alastair trailed clumsily behind us, clutching his bucket, as we progressed from fire to fire, launching bangers as we went. Now and then in the midst of battle he paused to pluck a helpful firework from his store, but he had not brought matches of his own and no one seemed inclined to light them for him. It was the best part of an hour later that we returned to our own waning fire. Mr Jencks was waiting. Father launched our rocket and we watched it carve a satisfying orange arc against the distant looming cooling towers. As Mr Jencks took the bucket of fireworks from Alastair I saw him look inside and glance up, throwing an unpleasant conspiratorial wink in Father's direction. I felt suddenly sorry for the boy at my side. I heard Mr Jencks say his mother had been waiting and they should get back to the car.

Chapter 10

Auntie Bessie had gone when we went home. The sky was already alive with rockets larger, noisier and more colourful than ours as grown-ups inherited what remained of Guy Fawkes night. I remember the smell of Father's cigarette as he walked back with us part of the way; how he suddenly stopped, saying he *needed to see to the fire*. At the top of the steps I looked back. He was standing on his own, staring across to Mr Harrison's greenhouses, not doing anything with the fire, which was almost out. I knew he did not want to come home.

Mother was in the kitchen waiting for us. She sponged the remains of blackened potato from Ian's face, laughing as he wriggled free, telling him to go and run the bath. She seemed changed – unaccountably engaged in a way I had not seen for many months. The only alcohol in the house, a bottle of *advocaat* last opened for some distant Christmas, stood on the flap of the yellow dresser, its stopper out. There were traces of eggy alcohol inside two sherry glasses that I had never before seen out of the cupboard. A chair with a cushion had been brought from the living room to make two side by side. Mother flopped down, smiling up at me, asking where Father had put himself. She sounded different, light-hearted in a way which made my heart thump at the thought she was starting one of her turns. I wondered whether she was perhaps a little drunk, but when she saw me glance at the bottle, she took my face between her hands, and said *you silly girl*, something she used to say as a sort of joke years ago when I was little. It was only as I pulled away, I saw the Wolverhampton Hospital Appointment Booklet lying on the kitchen floor, between the chairs, torn across in two. Father came in, making a fuss of locking the outside door, picking Ian up to take him to his bath. Mother asked him whether he'd like a cup of tea. He must have seen the booklet on the floor, but did not pick it up.

I know Mother never completed the remaining sessions of *unmodified* ECT. What I shall never know is how that came about and what those two warring sisters discussed that bonfire night; how they came to make their peace. Perhaps Mother had the easier path in that - she had already declared her jealous indignation on that dreadful day we visited Ashleigh Road. All that seemed justified by Father's inexplicable absence now: what was that, if not a confession of regret? It was Aunt Bessie who had the harder part to play. Father must have long since explained how Mother's pathetic show of poise that day had precipitated a terrible decline. She knew well enough how ill her sister was; acknowledging her part in bringing it about must have cost her dear.

More than an hour those sisters had sat side by side as we had wandered the smoky streets. Bess was the older by a year or two, but close enough to Dot to stir memories of rivalry in distant schoolgirl years. Perhaps there had been disputes over many another boy. All I know is now it had come to this: Dot possessed of nothing but her three golden boys and driven almost mad; Bess, a lonely widow, thoughtlessly consumed with envy for the nothing that consumed her sister's life. That must be why Alastair had come. Alastair, forced to flaunt a gift he must have known we would resent. Poor over-dressed Alastair, plucked from his distant school, recruited to fight his mother's hopeless cause like another boy sent out dressed in pom-pom shoes.

*

A few weeks after the Christmas holidays I was kept back after my mathematics class and told to go to another room to see Mr Bonar, someone who played the organ every morning at Assembly. He also taught older boys *calculus*, a subject apparently so demanding that unruly howls of protest from his class often disturbed the whole school. He was waiting for me in a room that still smelt of the dozen or so huge boys that had come shouting past me on the staircase as I made my timid way up to this distant foreign realm. The blackboard behind him confirmed my worst fears – it was dense with cabalistic signs.

Mr Bonar was allegedly Scottish, although apart from an occasional harassed squeak he sounded much the same as the other masters. He seemed more nervous than me, taking his time to reach an opening sally: *We gather you're not progressing in mathematics, Kennedy.* That ominous *we* again, as potent as many a secret smile - confirmation, if such were needed, that Kennedy's descent in the ranks of 4S had reached a wider audience. Perhaps, after all, The Pot regretted finding that extra desk. But he seemed a kindly chap, this Bonar man, and was already framing a softer set of words: *We think, all things considered, it might be best.* There was comfort of a kind in that word *might*, something to cling to, although he still seemed painfully unwilling to declare who *we* were, and exactly *what* they thought best. Indeed, when the sentence finally emerged I barely registered its sense: *We think it might be best if you take your year again.* Startled by my stricken face he seemed instantly to regret the words he'd left hanging in the stuffy silent room. After a long silence he feebly added, *You'd better discuss this with your father,* turning aside, enormously relieved to have his blackboard to clean. He was still rubbing when I shuffled out into the corridor.

*

Perhaps because I was closer to Mother than the others, I never accepted that her recovered spirits would endure. There was something contrived in the way she would laugh more than she need, and laugh too loud; something too theatrically rehearsed in the way she affected to draw Father into games with us he had never played. I came to believe her recovery was never more than a pretence born of fear of the misguided efforts to make her well. Perhaps she collapsed in despair once we had left for school but, if so, she hid it well, even allowing me to miss the bus the morning as I poured out Mr Bonar's cruel attempt to blight my life. Better to leave the school altogether than join a class I had already left behind. I remember she smiled at my passion, saying it was hardly the end of the world, but adding she would write and explain we had recently had some difficult days.

She must have written to great effect because calamity was forestalled. I did not repeat the year, but joined two other boys in desperate straits and found myself closeted with Mr Bonar twice a week for *extra algebra*. This timid little man could easily have made common cause with Mr Furnivall himself. At that hour's end we not only knew how to use the quadratic formula, but understood its derivation with two simple drawings on how to *complete the square*. That hour of patient geometry – not difficult at all - opened magic casements for three clumsy boys, unveiling what months of Mr Carter's pointless hammering had failed to reveal. Even now I remember hearing myself say *it's b over two squared*, wondering who was saying the words and how he came to know. I walked on air that morning.

*

As we moved into spring that year, Mother seemed herself again. She made us breakfast, packed our satchels for school, commanded baths when we were inclined to resist, scolded us when we went too far. Even let the blood rush scarlet to my face one tragic morning, taking me aside to say I should leave my bedclothes in a better state and *I should use my hand if I had to*. Shocking to realise she somehow knew my shameful secret - that growing up was proving a troublesome affair, filling my fourteen-year-old dreams with luxuries I would happily have lived without. Although it was cousin Alastair who brought about my first encounter with what passed for the reality of sex in those distant days.

There had been far fewer visits to Solihull after Mother recovered and the occasions more formally planned, even to the point of invitations filled out on cards that clearly had been printed for other times. That particular *luncheon* – so declared - we ate in style. It was May of my fourteenth year, sitting on hard chairs with whispered prompts as to which of a bewildering choice of forks to use. That meal was marked in more ways than one - an immense and perilous object, termed a *Gravy Boat*, proving far too large for Ian to hold.

It never seemed to rain in Solihull. The windows opened onto wooden rustic boxes packed with pink carnations and gillyflowers filling the dining room with the opulent scent of musk and clove. The meal over, to my surprise I was not told to get down, but sat, enraptured, as Aunt Bessie sang to us from the *Dream of Gerontius*, not knowing who Gerontius was or, for that matter, why he dreamed.

Alastair and I picked out tunes on the piano most of that afternoon. Although neither of us had the faintest idea how to play the instrument, he passed on to me the progression of keys, C A F G, that some boy at his school had shown him. We filled the house with anarchic improvisations over these familiar notes, Alastair pounding them out in enthusiastic octaves in the bass. We were enormously pleased with ourselves; so much so I barely noticed that our visit had almost strayed into evening with no particular preparations to go back home.

Mother called us in for *tea*, a meal that did not exist at that hour in Ocker Hill and seemed to have no other purpose but keep us occupied while the dining room, now out of bounds, was prepared for some other, more demanding, feast. Father, who had spent his afternoon with Mr Jencks battling some problem in the greenhouses, appeared as tea ended, telling us to go upstairs and change. It was only then that Mother explained there were clean things to wear in the bedroom, and that we would be staying for the night.

*

All I recall of that evening event was the magical presence of girls. At that time, girls of my age were only to be found in uniform. But not these. Unlike any to be found in Ocker Hill; even unlike the girls you met in giggling huddles on the bus to Dudley. Possibly they were like the mysterious creatures locked in the inaccessible redoubt of Stourbridge High School but we were not permitted ever to be close enough to know. This particular girl said her name was Rowena, which is all I will ever know of her, since we never met again. She came boldly up to where I stood alone and asked me to get an ashtray for her cigarette. At least fourteen and a half, dressed in becoming black and sophisticated beyond belief. She perched herself on the arm of a chair and asked me in a lilting laconic voice how I came to know Al, adding that my brother reminded her of Frank Sinatra. I had never heard of Frank Sinatra and it took me some time to realise that Al was my cousin, now occupied on the terrace outside with all the boys who had arrived with Solihull's *demi-monde*. I had been abandoned to do the best I could with Rowena's brutal inquisition.

She collected her audience and pressed me to tell her my interests and how I passed my time in the holidays. I could see that the innocent reply, *the works of Lord Dunsany*, although roughly correct, had failed to impress and recklessly added *and repairing crystal sets*, risking an immediate demand for technical detail. But I was not pressed to justify the boast. She explained she had meant, *did I ski at all?* a word that had so far escaped my lexicon. Fortunately, when I said I didn't know what the word meant the gales of laughter were for my dry wit in the Frank Sinatra style.

I confess the barely-clad Rowena filled my thoughts that night in my unfamiliar bed. Ruminations in which sex played little part. In humiliating a callow schoolboy before these perfumed creatures of the night, Aunt Bessie's intention had been that Alastair would come off best. In the event, there had not even been a contest - he had run away. I did not even think ill of her, because without conscious effort I had acquitted myself better than she would ever know. Discovering my dry wit had been compensation enough.

*

Towards the end of that school year, Stuart came home armed with a cricket bat, much used and bound with grimy tape, together with a single, slightly deformed, leather cricket ball. He refused to say how he had acquired these treasures, but we guessed they had been euphemistically "rescued" from wherever the groundsman had abandoned them. We began playing a unique form of the game of cricket involving only three players and a generally grassless pitch fashioned from playable parts of the tiny garden. The wickets were placed of necessity close to the wall dividing the garden from the alleyway that ran down to the street, meaning that play was largely restricted to the on-side. Since Ian was the only one of us capable of regularly hitting the ball, the game settled to a format in which I would field to Stuart's bowling, Ian doing his best to loft the ball to the roof of the shed defining the mid-wicket boundary, that shot counting as a six. On this particular afternoon, a spectacular drive from a fast delivery found the meat of the ancient bat and flew gracefully over the bowler's head. The sound of distant breaking

86

glass reached us as the ball passed through the living room window where Father was last seen reading his newspaper. We stood frozen in paralysed immobility.

Father appeared shortly afterwards, still wearing his slippers, his face red with fury. He had the offending ball in his hand. He stood for a moment getting his balance before throwing it further than we thought possible, over the garden wall beyond the metal fencing of the Power Station grounds. We heard a dull metallic clink before it thudded into distant inaccessible weeds. Pushing Ian aside, he snatched the bat from his hands, and began pounding it in a frenzy against the brickwork of the mid-off boundary, on and on, until the handle finally split apart. Throwing what was left of our bat to the ground he walked away.

Mr Harrison's efforts at a replacement bat were almost comically inadequate. Fashioned from a single sad piece of raw timber he said it was the best he could manage, adding he realised it could not be used with a proper cricket ball, but since we no longer had one, we might be able to play with a tennis ball. The bat was far too short and we only persisted with cricket to punish Father, knowing only too well that the fact we had turned to Mr Harrison for this pitiful relief had consumed him with remorse.

Chapter 11

We refused to speak to Father after the breaking of the bat. For the others, the mutiny soon petered out but I found him harder to forgive, and the silence of a few days lease ran on into far longer periods in which we barely exchanged words. Mother knew, of course, the true source of my hurt. Father had all too easily recruited Stuart to his cause with a querulous whine over supper that first night: *it's them who should say sorry, what did they expect?* She would not look at either of them, staring intently down at her plate. For my part, watching Stuart smile as Father made a joke about Mr Harrison's carpentry skills roused me to fury. I was reminded of Stuart's secretive, enigmatic expression the morning after Mother's sudden illness the night of the gas. Even then, the awareness that he would never tell me what he knew seemed like a chasm between us. How could he desert us so casually now, letting Father secure a victory he knew was undeserved? Watching Mother's face and remembering the days when we had worked on the puppet heads together - something Father could still barely bring himself to acknowledge - I realised she too was busy securing a kind of victory of her own. It came about a week later as she cheerfully called us down to breakfast, shouting *come and see what your father has done.* There was a cricket bat propped against the kitchen wall, its braided handle expensively marked with three dark bands. The brand-new smell of linseed oil filled the room. Father was not there, he must have already left for work. The bat rested where it was for days, untouched against the wall, until Mother took it away and left it in his shed. Father never mentioned it and I cannot recall playing cricket at home ever again.

*

Stuart had started taking piano lessons at the start of the new school year. His teacher was Mr Harrison's son, the soldier-godfather of my christening. The lesson itself took place on Saturday afternoon. At around tea-time Stuart would dash into the front room, where Mother's piano lived, collect his music from where it had lain for a week inside the padded piano stool, and walk next door for his lesson. Lessons rarely lasted more than a few minutes, the pupil reappearing to explain that he had been dismissed because he needed more practice. He would then return to the front room and bang out a few desultory chords before reappearing to finish his tea. No fee was levied for this futile ritual although our meal was invariably accompanied through the wall we shared in common with our neighbour next door by a ferocious rendition of one of Schubert's *impromptus* – the one in E flat. At first, we took this high velocity performance as some kind of frustrated revenge for the lost lesson, but we eventually discovered it was, in fact, the work of my raspberry cane friend who had by then impressively graduated from her days with scales.

I did my homework in the front room, sitting at a tiny bureau next to the window, and got into the habit, once I'd finished, of seating myself at the piano and attempting to decipher the music Stuart had left in the piano seat. A large flimsy booklet of about twenty pages, the music itself encased in boxes decorated with coloured pictures of elfin grots, imps and fairies. The first piece, entitled *The March of the Goblins*, had so few notes that I eventually mastered it sufficiently to arrive at an approximation to the sounds Stuart produced during his rare efforts at practice. I was aided in this activity by an article on the piano in *The Children's Encyclopedia* - the only use I ever found for a solemn weekly publication Mother demanded we read before granting us access to *The Beano*.

It is difficult to practise the piano in secret and even Father must have been aware of my efforts. Had we been on speaking terms I would have asked him if I could also have lessons with Mr Harrison, but we were not, and I left it to Mother to make the request. She duly conveyed his refusal, telling me to stop being silly and speak to my father properly, adding that if I asked him myself he might well say yes. My rejoinder was to begin work on the next piece in the book, something Stuart had yet to confront. This absurd musical competition came to define yet another proxy battleground on which my parents continued their war for my soul.

Since there was nothing in the *Encyclopedia* about how to time the designated notes, my relentless pounding of *The Pixie's Polka* was finally too much even for Father and he burst in, ordering me to stop making such a noise *and use the soft pedal*. This technical refinement had escaped me up to that point, although I took the fact that he had spoken to me as a kind of victory. I was secretly impressed that he would know about the workings of the piano's pedals - even more so when I discovered that one of them did indeed muffle the sound. I had not appreciated, of course, the part the next-door neighbours played in the matter. Schubert had been more than audible in 160, Leabrook Road for more weeks than we could remember; my own less fluent efforts at the *Pixie's Polka* had surely tormented the inhabitants of number 161 for much the same time. This was confirmed shortly afterwards, Mother saying that she had met Mr Furnivall in the fish shop and he wondered whether Alan could profit from piano lessons. When this news was conveyed to Father he made the fatal error of saying he wouldn't have two of us going next door for lessons and making fools of ourselves. Mother sprang her trap, ingenuously asking were there not piano lessons at the Grammar School on Saturdays – perhaps it was best if I enrolled in those? She triumphantly commissioned me to enquire about the fees that very day.

Mother came with me for the piano audition, my spirited rendition of the *Pixie's Polka* making redundant her explanation that I had been, to that point, wholly self-taught. I was assessed by the school organist, a distinguished musician, who was obviously having difficulty keeping a straight face and even more obviously reluctant to take on a kind of inverted musical *idiot savant*. Thinking it would be an end to the matter and allow Mother to safely take me away, he adopted a tragic air and explained that I was, unfortunately, too old to be prepared for the Associated Board examinations. He had not reckoned with the power of ignorance: since I had never heard of the Associated Board, my request to learn to play without taking examinations left him completely foxed. There was a long pause, during which he wrinkled his face, apparently deep in mental calculation. Finally, defeated, he mumbled that he would see what could be done with me, turning to Mother in one final appeal for confirmation of the incredible fact that I might want to play *for my own pleasure*. We went home on the bus together, Mother clutching the receipt for ten lessons paid in advance.

My reluctant teacher could hardly have imagined I would be making my public concert debut at the piano in only a few short months.

*

Piano lessons coincided with my accession to the first of the two fifth forms in the school, years in which science boys spent Saturday mornings in the chemistry lab. Working in pairs, we were allocated benches for the year and given access to sufficient lethal liquids to put an end to Stourbridge many times over. My own shared supplies of nitric, sulphuric and hydrochloric acids inevitably left their mark and it was a rare piano lesson when some modest accident had not rendered my fingers bright yellow from nitric acid or stained black with silver nitrate. Although instructed in the operation of the fume cupboards, clothes impregnated with hydrogen sulphide probably added a memorable pungency to the lessons.

Piano playing was generally considered a highly suspect, and possibly sissy, activity by members of the science community and I found myself recruited into a little band of malcontents. Bashforth and Brown were also reluctant scientists, creatures after my own heart. Bashforth, my pom-pom saviour, had long since declared himself unsuited to school altogether, intending to leave as soon as he could escape his parents' thrall. To that end he had already committed himself to the clarinet and engaged in clandestine lessons, at his own expense, at a secret address in Stourbridge. So far as I recall, he did no other work whatsoever, and progressed through the school despite failing every examination put in his way. Brown, albeit barely fifteen, posted weekly packages of poems to periodicals and seemed undaunted when his own reply-paid envelope invariably brought them back. Without conscious effort we formed ourselves into a trio of dissidents casting envious eyes at The Pot's favoured literary boys for whom Virgil was no longer a mystery.

My music teacher was as good as his word, leavening a diet of Burgmüller's studies with a selection of elementary pieces by Bach and Schumann which I executed very badly, but resolutely for my own pleasure, - and completely without thought for the Associated Board. After a few weeks hacking at problems Anna Magdalena Bach had struggled with two hundred years earlier, I eventually acquired an audience. Mother got into the habit of slipping into the room to listen to me practise. It was the time of day when the others would be already noisily devouring whatever was available on the wireless. At first, I thought Mother came as silent consolation for missed episodes of *Take it From Here*, but I soon realised she had another reason, defining my lonely piano lessons as a subversive rejoinder to Father who never mentioned them since he refused to acknowledge they even took place. If there were two camps, I suppose I was recruited to my mother's side. In truth, however, I soon had more pressing musical concerns.

As Christmas approached, two of the three dissidents, Brown and Kennedy, volunteered to help with the School Concert and were assigned the task of issuing programmes at the door – reluctantly, because science boys rarely involved themselves in artistic matters and mischief was suspected. The role of Programme Boy, however, brought me the right to attend rehearsals and watch Bashforth perform on his clarinet. I joined rehearsals soon after his engagement to play what the Programme described as a *popular song* in his allotted slot of time. To discover him mid-flow in violent dispute with his accompanist, Mr Bonar. I was never to know the cause of their quarrel. Apart from a clash of artistic temperaments, I think the problem was grounded in the fact that the tempo Bashforth had selected, while prudent given his competence on the clarinet, was about half that indicated on the printed music. The upshot was Bashforth angrily dismissing Mr Bonar and declaring that Kennedy, who he knew to be a piano student, had agreed to accompany him.

*

The Austin Big Seven, polished for the occasion, had one of its rare excursions on the night of the Concert, Father deciding to ferry his family in style to Stourbridge. In the event, I went ahead to prepare for my programme duties and to meet with the piano tuner for instruction in the use of the school's instrument, a concert grand Bösendorfer which, apart from extremely rare public appearances, passed its days like a sacred relic untouched beneath a thick felt blanket. The tuner sat me down, wound a handle in the seat until I said stop, asked whether I was comfortable, noted something in a little book and called to the next performer in the queue. He shouted after me to go and wash my hands; fortunately, he did not ask me to play anything.

Bashforth had secured the right to rehearse his performance in the Art Room where the battered upright piano reminded me of the one in the bagatelle bar in the Princes End pub of fond memory. It was extremely out of tune. By the time of our first rehearsal, I had practised the accompaniment (simplified edition) on Mother's piano for more than an hour each day for well over a month. Apart from a short passage in octaves, which I artfully reduced to single notes, I could easily match Bashforth's lugubrious tempo. The night of the concert we were virtually the first performers on stage. I remember standing in the wings, looking across the empty space at my lonely music perched on the piano. The boy at my side cranked a huge wheel, opening the curtains onto an excited buzz of chatter. A powerful wave of adolescent heat, cigarette smoke and perfume rose up to meet us. I caught a fleeting glimpse of The Pot in the front row with someone I assumed was Mrs Pot. Behind him, stretching back to the distant stained glass, was an audience containing more of the magical creatures of Stourbridge High than I had dared imagine existed. Sisters - approving or otherwise – were present in considerable numbers, some even sporting their Proustian summer boaters for the show. We were prodded out onto the stage, Bashforth and clarinet first.

I had slept very badly the night before, dreaming about a public performance of the *Pixie's Polka*, and anticipating catastrophe in all its guises. But none ensued. Bashforth's clarinet solo passed off well enough, if at a leisurely pace, and earned sufficient applause for him to bow before we both scuttled away, people already checking their Programmes to see what was next. Our first, and only, professional review appeared in *The Express and Star* two days later and ran to six words, one of which was *unhurried*; there was no mention of the accompanist, whose name, in fact, did not appear in the Programme.

*

At half-time I made my way into the Hall in search of the seat Mother said she would keep for me. Working my way round, I was waylaid by Major Delauney. He found Father and shook his hand, leaving his other resting on my shoulder in a proprietorial fashion. Across the aisle, a group of High School girls was watching the elegant Major as he clicked open his cigarette case, offering it to Father. I realised I, in turn, had been watching a girl standing a little apart from the others. Watching for some time, in fact; curiously unconscious of a secret pleasure. It was only as I realised she was also looking at me that I felt I should look away, knowing it was rude to stare. Perhaps she had the same thought because she suddenly turned aside smiling to herself. But not before we had, it seemed, been close enough to touch. My heart inexplicably pounding, I realised Major Delaunay was still talking to Father: *Deep chap, your son. I got to know him in Paris. I was talking just now to the Head – he said he had no idea Kennedy played the piano. What did you think?* I will never know if Father intended a reply because Mother barely gave him time. My heart still racing at the thought of those distant eyes, I was forced to listen as she launched into the story of her treasured musical box. Launched at such extraordinary length that a somewhat bewildered Major Delauney eventually remembered someone he had to speak to urgently. I sat between Mother and Father for the rest of that night, cocooned in an exquisite aura of satisfaction, entirely unconscious of the rest of the show, my mind filled with images of dark hair under a straw hat; and dark eyes.

We walked to where the car was waiting to take us home, Mother going a little ahead. As she reached out to open her door, Father called, *let him sit in the front.* She was in high spirits in the back of the car, calling *Drive on James,* although only Ian laughed. She leaned forward, pulling my shoulder, saying *you did well. I knew you would,* adding loudly for Father's benefit, *Didn't I tell you?* I glanced across at

Father who said, *sit back Dorothy, for God's sake, you'll have us over.* But Mother had started again, tugging at my shoulder. *Who was that girl eyeing you, our Alan? She's an eyeful herself. Did you see her eying our Alan, Bob?* She turned away, asking Ian if he wanted to play *I spy* like he used to when he was little, and *does anyone fancy a little song?* The sense of supressed menace in the car seemed to annoy her and she leaned back, humming loudly to herself for a while before suddenly saying *I told you he'd do well. And he did, and he did, and he did, and he did.* I tried to turn round, feeling sick, my heart thumping. The car wavered as Father leaned across me, reaching for something he could not find, his face close to my own. A kind of despairing whisper; perhaps he wasn't even aware I heard: *I forgot your mother's medicine.* It was the first seizure in two years. Mother sitting rigid, hard against the leather of the seat, her eyes closed.

Chapter 12

Mother stayed in bed the following day, declaring she would not see the doctor even if he came to the house so it was no use asking him; it was the heat in that school hall that had brought it on, anyway it had passed and she would be getting up. Stuart was a medical student now, although only in his first year, and Father spent much of the morning consulting him in the kitchen, with no very definite outcome. Since neither of them seemed to want to talk to her and Mother had not yet got up, I visited her and sat on the little padded stool at the foot of the bed, hoping she would talk about my piano playing and the concert. Artlessly pressed to agree that Bashforth had done really well with his clarinet, she said she could not remember that bit, although she was sure it was very nice, and was Bashforth my particular friend? Eyes restlessly darting from object to object as if to remember what purpose they served, gave the lie to the apparent calm of the placid face turned towards me. Trying again with my time at the Bösendorfer, she stared at me for a while, finally mumbling, *I'm not sure I remember that. It'll come back. Was it nice?*

Not that she had forgotten everything. She brightened when I mentioned Major Delauney. *Oh, I remember him. And who might that girl be, the one staring so?* Put to denying I had even noticed a girl, I remembered the impudent tilt of a straw boater, dark hair and deep dark eyes. Feeling my pulse rise, I found myself blushing, my face precipitating yet more interrogation, this time her tone teasing, not friendly at all, until she took my desperate glance at the door as vindication, calling after me as I slipped out, *there's nothing wrong you saying. She's not the first, I'll be bound.*

*

My piano teacher greeted me with a broad smile at my first lesson after the holiday, saying he never knew he had been harbouring a secret star; he would certainly have come if he'd known I would be playing at the concert. Seeing I had inadvertently pulled out the music for the concert from my briefcase, where it had a permanent home alongside Anna Magdalena Bach, he spread it out on the fretted music stand of the piano and demanded a performance. Without Bashforth at my side, the piece seemed sadly diminished, but I stumbled through it, aware of him pacing the room in his usual fashion. He made no comment at the end, simply leaning over me and marking the sheet with his pencil in two places, *no need to correct the E natural here, it was intended. I can see why you changed it, but whoever wrote it wanted the dissonance with the clarinet. You'll have to get used to dissonances.* I nodded earnestly, revelling in this, my first, professional exchange and certainly willing to get used to things; although he was surely well aware I had very little idea what he was talking about. He handed me my music back saying, *I'd like to show you something. Leave your things here, we won't be long.* Putting his hat and coat on, he signalled for me to follow.

Piano lessons were held in rooms above a music shop virtually next door to the school. I followed him as far as the main gates and through a side door. At the top of a flight of stone stairs I recognised the narrow entrance through which Mr Bonar emerged each morning to play the organ for Assembly. We were at the organ desk: a bewildering array of illuminated tabs, three keyboards, a long polished bench and a radiating pedalboard. All bigger and vastly more complicated than the instrument that accommodated Mr Bannister every Sunday, tucked away behind the choir stalls of St Mark's.

I was not to know, of course, but that brief hour, sitting awe-struck on the bench alongside my music teacher (on condition I kept my feet away from the pedals) changed my life. I would never make a pianist, he said, you must start early for that and, even then, few pianists rise to the challenge that the sound of a piano can be modulated in an infinity of ways. He was sorry, because he could see I had a facility and was willing to work. That was why he had brought me here - the organ is not concerned with the actions of whoever is playing it. Certainly, a peerless musical instrument but also a machine. A machine that responds to amateur and professional alike. He pressed one of the tabs and pointed to the second of the three keyboards: *See for yourself. Touch counts for nothing. Press the key however you like, you'll get the same sound.* I tentatively pressed the key two or three times, a sound like a soft flute echoed in the empty Hall behind.

Move over, I'll play you something and you'll see what an organ can do.

And he did. I went home bewitched by Bach's great *Passacaglia*, its theme softly opening with the pedals alone and building to a crescendo which shook the walls. That was the day I set my heart on mastering an extraordinary machine that was not one but dozens of different instruments; determined to join the company of those who had made such sounds for five hundred years or more. There was only one obstacle – I must secure access to an organ for practice. Hardly an obstacle, my teacher said, *just ask your father to arrange it with the organist at your church. Who knows, in a few years he may take you on as his deputy!* How little he knew of the feuds of Ocker Hill. Father had not exchanged words with Mr Bannister for many a year. He was not going to start now - not on my behalf.

Inevitably, it fell to Mother to bring an end to my dream, walking together one rainy morning down Leabrook Road as far as the cobbler's shop to make the fatal request. It was not a happy encounter. Mr Bannister received the news I was taking organ lessons at school in silence, turning his back on us to fiddle with a pile of boxes. Mother tried again, her words petering out: *He's come for permission to practise ... at St Mark's ... the church ... at the organ.* He seemed about to say something, then changed his mind, coming round the counter to turn the little *Open* label hanging down inside the door, *If you're done missus, we're closed.* He waited at the door until we shuffled out into the street. Conveyed to Father, the refusal only confirmed the worst of all he had ever believed of his enemy, but when Mother asked him to take it up with the vicar, he shook his head; *he wasn't crawling to anybody.*

Since Mother had already paid, I began my organ lessons, nonetheless, but in a hopeless, halting, fashion, with only a piano for practice and doing the best I could with the hour's free time I was allowed on the school organ. Without an instrument to play, it was obvious to teacher and pupil alike that my first ten lessons would be my last - the venture was doomed. That this catastrophe was triumphantly eluded, albeit in a most peculiar and serpentine way, I owe wholly to the Archbishop of Canterbury himself. As you will discover soon enough.

*

One Saturday afternoon I arrived home to discover Mr Furnivall in the living room, deep in conversation with Father. Since the room was full of smoke, they seemed to have been talking for some time, and about me, because I was greeted by Father with an ambiguous, *here he is now*, and waved into a chair while they returned *sotto voce* to an apparently intense discussion. I strained to follow a curiously conspiratorial conversation, which seemed to be about the installation of a new Dean at Lichfield Cathedral, an event apparently to be celebrated – together with the cathedral's new roof - by a service attended by the Archbishop of Canterbury.

The television broadcast of the Coronation of the Queen had revealed a surprising public appetite for choral religious ceremony on a grand scale. We were, in fact, surely the last generation to offer entirely innocent ears to patriotic works by Elgar, Parry, Walton, Stanford, Purcell and many an English other. An intricate ceremonial, albeit barely visible on millions of tiny domestic television sets, had struck the nation like a thunderclap and people wanted more. A wish about to be satisfied, at least in Lichfield, by a colossal ecumenical service bringing together the youth of the Diocese in their many hundreds. The word *together* had been the Archbishop's: the children of the Midlands were to learn the evils of schism. How long had it been that Methodists had broken away from their mother church? High time to heal the rift.

It was only as Mr Furnivall reached this point that my part in this theological debate was made clear. Apparently, all the Methodist Chapels in the region had been invited to join a competition to find boys capable of reading the lessons to a cathedral congregation. That they might also have found girls for the job was not considered, church at that time being a male affair. Masculine or not, the challenge had defeated the Methodist children of Ocker Hill, whose impenetrable accent rendered them unintelligible to all but close relatives. Facing defeat, Mr Furnivall had come at the prompting of his daughter, to suggest one of the Kennedy boys might somehow play a part. Now it was true that raspberry canes had by then been long supplanted by the appeal of a trim straw hat, but my heart beat a little faster, nonetheless. Knowing Stuart was too old and Ian too young, she must have calculated that if it was to be anyone, it would be me.

At this point Mr Furnivall leaned a little closer to Father, glancing nervously at the door as if, however improbably, some irate vicar might even now burst into the room to denounce a diabolical ecclesiastical plot - for a plot was certainly what he had in mind. Not on the scale of a Medici, to be sure, but these things must start somewhere and Mr Furnivall's starting point was young Alan presented in the competition as a Methodist. *Who knows, he might be selected and Ocker Hill would have its day of fame. Where was the harm?* Father had already admitted that the vicar of St Mark's – known to be High Church by the secret Catholic buttons on his cassock - had announced that he wanted no part in any such ecumenical heresy. Given the church was not involved, why not let the chapel play its part? It seemed a shame to let the chance go begging.

Father turned to me: *Would you be interested?* It had been a day or two since he had spoken to me and I made the most of my right of reply, aiming into the blank space between the two of them to explain that although I attended St Mark's on Sunday, I also went to the Methodist film show on Thursday, *and did this count?* The admission was seized on by Mr Furnivall as so close to a religious conversion as to make no difference. Tossing a conspiratorial, *that's a point, you know,* in Father's direction, he added, as if Hitchcock himself had settled my faith, *and he's a regular, I can vouch for that myself.*

Sworn to secrecy, a few days later, the faux Methodist was ferried to Lichfield by Mr Furnivall himself. To sit among rows of awe-struck boys before the chancel steps of a vast gothic cathedral. A man in long black robes told us the piece of paper in his hand contained a few words from the New Testament. We were to pass the paper along, each standing in turn to call out our name and church, then read it out aloud, *in a nice clear voice*. About an hour later, having heard *and the greatest of these is charity* some fifty times or more, there was a lengthy pause for muttered communion among a group of men who had been sitting in a side chapel. Eventually I heard my name called and joined a little group of boys for the second round.

I climbed a flight of very steep stairs to declaim the opening of St John's gospel written out on a piece of paper and pinned to the pulpit desk. The man in black had seated himself below me among ranks of empty chairs. I had been the only Methodist chosen and I watched a second conspiracy unfold inexorably before my eyes. This one not unlike a card game played many years before. I would do my best - and in truth I read quite well - but other forces had been at work. I was fated to win.

I went home possessed of elaborate instructions on the timing, rehearsal, and reading of the second lesson from the Old Testament. My allotted task: *Genesis* chapter eight, the story of Noah, the raven and the dove.

> And it came to pass at the end of forty days, that Noah opened the window of the ark which he had made: and he sent forth a raven, which went forth to and fro, until the waters were dried up from off the earth. Also he sent forth a dove from him, to see if the waters were abated from off the face of the ground; But the dove found no rest for the sole of her foot, and she returned unto him into the ark, for the waters were on the face of the whole earth: then he put forth his hand, and took her, and pulled her in unto him into the ark. And he stayed yet other seven days; and again he sent forth the dove out of the ark; and the dove came in to him in the evening; and, lo, in her mouth was an olive leaf pluckt off: so Noah knew that the waters were abated from off the earth. And he stayed yet other seven days; and sent forth the dove; which returned not again unto him any more.

Mr Lamb's fifth-form physics class had already inducted me into the maxim that absence of proof was not proof of absence and it seemed clear that Noah had placed far too much credence on the results of a very weak experiment. Unfortunately, it was difficult to see how I could inject a measure of scepticism on the point into my reading. On the other hand, it had been raining for weeks across the Midlands and it occurred to me that a little emphasis on the phrase, *for the waters were on the face of the whole earth*, would not be out of place. I set about rehearsing my sixty-five seconds with this nuance in mind. Rehearsals took place from the more modest pulpit of Ocker Hill Methodist Chapel, where I was conducted by Mr Furnivall himself, twice a week. It was my first encounter with the sacred part of that building. Positioned directly above the hall where the film shows took place, the space was more lofty than I had imagined, with the appearance of something between a school and a theatre, with stairs rising right and left at the back to give access to a tiered balcony. Rows of austere polished benches on either side of a central aisle faced a long table bearing a single wooden cross but no candles. The place seemed altogether too well-lit for any kind of church, with huge undecorated windows on either side. But it was not the disconcerting light that had caught my attention - behind the table-altar, partly hidden by a screen, the decorated metal pipes of an organ rose almost to the ceiling. My first rehearsal finished, I asked if I could look at the organ desk, explaining to Mr Furnivall that I was taking organ lessons.

Of course. Would you like to play it? I'll show you how to switch the blower on. Why don't you practise on it? You can get the key from the caretaker.

And with these words, a Methodist was born.

*

The deckle-edged invitation to Mother and Father arrived in an elaborate gilt envelope a few days later, together with a reminder that his Grace the Archbishop hoped to have time to meet them and to that end they should remain seated after the service until the congregation had left. Up to now, Father's proudest personal encounter had been with Lord Baden Powell at a Scouting Jamboree many years before and he had always regretted being too young to remember whether he had actually shaken hands with the great man. He clearly relished the prospect of rectifying this omission with no less a personage than an Archbishop. Notoriously punctual, he delivered the three of us to Lichfield Cathedral in the freshly polished Austin on the day of my reading. He was several hours too early, hurrying off in search of the Kennedy's appointed seats before they had even been labelled.

I felt sorry for the reserve reader seated at my side at the foot of the pulpit. A cheerful looking boy of about my own age, he had no doubt rehearsed as assiduously as me and done his Christian best to limit the calamities that might have precipitated my absence to a sore throat or, *in extremis*, a single broken leg. He did his best to smile as I joined him before the service began. He seemed more nervous than me as we waited our turn, eyes glued to the tiny lamp which would wink to signal my ascent of the pulpit. Possibly, even at this late hour, he nursed hopes that I might funk it and push him ahead to take my place. If so, he was disappointed. The reading passed off well, even to the tiny ripple of approval for the theatrical pause on reaching the bit about the waters covering the face of the earth. The congregation had already begun a hymn as I made my way down the pulpit stairs to be taken in hand by a man in a red gown. As he led me and my shadow to our allotted places in the choir stalls he patted my back and whispered, *good show.*

Lichfield Cathedral is made in threes: three great doors and three spires; above all, three stupendous stained-glass windows crown its vaulted aisle, the equal of those of Notre Dame. I was to pass the rest of the service sightlessly staring through this medieval glass, pride in my success slowly evaporating as the guilty consequences of my deception bore in on me. Confronted with news of my sudden religious conversion, what was Vicar Bell going to say? I already knew what Mother would say: in Ocker Hill to declare yourself a Methodist was to join the other side. She never defined these sides, but was certain that it would never do - not for a Stourbridge boy. And pondering this point, I realised the true source of my anguish: the certainty that a girl with deep dark eyes would also not approve. And as that thought invaded my mind, I cemented the guilty resolution that Stourbridge need never know.

*

After the service, Mother was reluctant to come to the meeting with the Archbishop, declaring herself content to stay where she was: nobody would be interested in seeing her; and she was tired; and did we think there were toilets anywhere? She came eventually, as we knew she would, Father's final desperate cry echoing down the empty aisle, *come on Dorothy, for God's sake, don't make a fuss.*

As we hurried through a side door a tall man in a huge red cape broke away from a discussion with my fellow orators and their parents and swooped down on us, asking whether we had got ourselves lost. Father secured more of a handshake than he could have expected, the Archbishop hanging on with one hand and pulling me into his little group with the other. His voice boomed out: *So you're the little Methodist with a taste for theatre*, then, seeing my sudden stricken face, hurrying on with, *no, no, you read it very well. Worth the effort to make Noah interesting.* But any hopes I may have harboured of a brief discussion of experimental physics were dashed on hearing the one question I had prayed he would never ask. He turned to Mother who was already readying herself to leave. *You must be proud of your boy. How long has he been a Methodist?* She stood for a long time considering a reply, finally blurting into his bewildered face. *Oh, you'll have to ask Bob about that. He arranged it all.*

Chapter 13

It was a silent drive home and Mother went straight to bed, saying she was tired out. Stuart had made neatly piled tomato sandwiches for us as a celebration supper, spoiling the effect by eating one because we were very late. Father put some on a plate and went upstairs with Mother's bottle of medicine. Ian had already taken his sandwich and gone out to play, leaving me alone with Stuart. Perhaps the drama of the day had loosened my tongue but I began talking about how Mother had changed since her attacks began. I found myself reminding him of the day she had played all the parts in my Punch and Judy show herself. That was when she had been an actress in the play about Connie Fately and she had made the three of us sit on the floor to be her audience. How she squeezed her nose when the crocodile said *that's the way to do it* and ended up laughing until she couldn't stop. Mother was always laughing then. It seemed a lifetime ago. I had reminded her the other day of how she had painted the crocodile for me and she said she couldn't remember anything about a crocodile. It was like talking to a stranger.

I poured my heart out to Stuart that evening, hoping to bring him to admit that he too was ashamed of the muddled, shambling, garrulous person that Mother had become. He heard me out in silence, finally saying, *it's the phenobarbital*, coldly handing the word across the table like some solemn medical talisman, then, seeing my face, adding *they are looking into it*, as consolation. I could see he had wanted to say *we*, but that single imperious *they* shut me out just as effectively. And realising how he had let me prattle on like a child talking about puppet shows, I felt myself reddening with anger.

*

It must have been a few weeks later we were asked to stay behind after a class at school to hear from a master who appeared only once a week, occupying himself delivering something called Religious Instruction to a tiny group of earnest sixth-form boys. He seemed intimidated by a room bulging with scientists and we could barely hear him, but eventually we learned that the Headmaster had sanctioned his creating a chess club in the school. He finally got to the point - *could any of us play?* There was a general murmur of dissent; Brown, eager to escape and already half out of his seat, shook a world-weary head. As the master turned away, somewhat crestfallen, I raised my hand, prodding Bashforth to join me.

Strictly speaking, this sympathetic gesture had been something of an exaggeration. I could lay claim to an elementary grasp of the rules of the game but, in fact, I had never laid hands on a chess piece. Some months before, during a particularly rainy holiday, Father had cut out some tiny coloured images of chess pieces from a puzzle in the *Radio Times* and carefully glued them to the counters of the family draughts set. Starting with Stuart, he had then set out to teach us the rules of chess, persisting until each of us, in turn, proved capable of defeating him. In fact, his knowledge of the game was so rudimentary it was only a matter of hours before he lost to Stuart, at which point he withdrew, apparently satisfied; at least, I cannot recall their playing again. It took even less time for me to win and an embarrassingly brief interval before he lost his very first game against Ian, although by then, of course, both of us had had the advantage of watching him play. It was only as he conceded Ian's game that I realised why he had so laboriously defaced a perfectly usable set of draughts when he could have simply bought a box of chess pieces – they surely cost less than a cricket bat. It dawned on me that he had found the ideal means to signal he had no personal interest in the game at all, still less any interest in continuing to play with us. He wished simply to equip us to play a game he considered part of the more sophisticated world he had determined we were to inhabit – one that he would never know.

I joined the school's embryonic chess club with Bashforth one evening after school. It was held in the Art Room, already sanctified by our concert rehearsals. By then, the fever of innumerable games with Stuart and Ian had faded, along with most of the images gummed to the draughts, but despite the unique disadvantage that this was my first encounter with solid pieces, I held my own in the series of games

I was set to play. Not that any of these reached a conclusion: after twenty or so moves the master told us to stop, briefly examined the state of the board, and declared one or another player the victor. His mumbled account of how he arrived at these decisions, and why he was so sure, intrigued me and, although I had intended to go home, I stayed behind for my first lesson in the theory of chess. Apart from an encyclopaedic knowledge of the game this part-time master had the peculiar distinction of three Christian names and his initials spelled out the only name I ever knew him by. Tall and stooped, TELC was as timid as a rabbit and so extremely thin he appeared to inhabit his clothes rather than wear them. Nonetheless, he would have made common cause with Mr Furnival – both were born to teach. I sat spellbound that evening as he shifted pieces about on a magnetic board, explaining the apparently endless consequences of the first few moves of the Ruy Lopez opening, pausing now and then to reflect on the deeper nature of chess, urging us – above all - *never to think of it as a game.*

As is the way of such things, a passion for chess swept through the school over the ensuing months. Unused storage space under the Assembly Hall was emptied of accumulated clutter and equipped with two parallel rows of four desks, each with its own Staunton set. This cavernous cellar had no windows and probably should not have been occupied, but an open door provided just about enough air to breathe and lunchtime sandwiches were now eaten in cerebral silence, broken only by the sound of hysterical lunges at the levers of our brand-new chess clocks, almost certainly paid for by TELC himself. In my second year in the fifth form, I finally secured a place in the school team, never playing the top board, but certainly discovering that chess was not a game.

Organ lessons had already eaten into my free half-day on Saturday. The Chess Club was now to be added to a list of societies that consumed Wednesday afternoons: the Debating Society; The Music Society; and Brown's sporadic but intense meetings with fellow poets. I had, in effect, converted Wednesday into a normal school day. Most weeks, Ian would bear the message home that I would be late, but inevitably I arrived to find the congealed remains of my mid-day meal inside the long-extinguished stove. Less of a penalty than you may imagine, because, like many of my generation, I came to accept feeling slightly hungry as a permanent feature of school existence. It is hard to thrive on sandwiches and was no doubt painful for Mother to watch her gangly son's bony wrists emerge as he rapidly out-grew his clothes, but she was far too ill to offer more than half-hearted attempts to teach me the rudiments of cooking. I would sometimes arrive home to discover ingredients set out on the dresser, with instructions as to what to do with them, but even that well-meaning gesture fell victim to my irregular hours. Too tired to care, I was certainly too tired to cook. Altogether unaware of what awaited me, I was already falling ill.

*

It was no more than a few weeks later. My Saturday organ lesson finished, I walked down to the music shop to pay the bill for the rest of the term. A tall woman was standing inside the shop with her back to the counter, examining customers as they arrived. She waited until I had paid my bill then came across and asked whether my name was Kennedy, looking down at a piece of paper and adding *Alan Kennedy*, presumably to exclude other possible Kennedys that might be there. To put matters beyond all possible doubt she greeted my rather bewildered nod with: *Takes organ lessons … that right? Yes, I can see it's you.* She explained that she was a teacher at the High School and had come to ask me whether I would like to join a play-reading group: *six boys from your school and six girls from mine. We meet in your Headmaster's house two or three times each term. Did you know about it?*

She need not have asked: how could anyone at the school not have known about these mysterious play-readers? It did not take long to discover a society that had earned itself an almost mystical aura of exclusivity. It did not take long to discover the futility of trying to join: the means of access, should any exist, while not exactly secret, seemed frustratingly inaccessible. I stood confronted by this woman wondering whether this was not some strange joke contrived by Brown. She looked down at the top of my head, apparently puzzled by my silence, and tried again. Someone had had to leave the group.

It was Joan who had suggested my name to fill the gap. It was Joan who knew I would be here today. *What did I think?*

It seemed only then to occur to her that I had no idea who this *Joan* might be and she explained it was someone who had heard me reading the lesson at Lichfield. Joan had heard my voice and thought I would suit the play-readers. I would need my parents' permission, of course, because the group met in the evenings, but they would make sure I caught the last bus home. As I wondered how she knew which bus I caught, let alone which home I went to, she must also have realised she had said too much and seemed a little annoyed, rattling off that I'd better make up my mind because there were others who might want my place. She stepped back, eyeing me up and down. *We're doing "Arms and the Man" next. There'll be a part for you, but don't expect too much – we can't all play Hamlet.* Stammering back that I would be happy just to hold a spear earned a reluctant smile. She squeezed my arm, releasing me with: *Well, that's enough playing gooseberry for today.* As she reached the door of the shop, I saw a girl outside on the pavement waiting. The two of them walked away together.

*

I sat in a warm cloud of satisfaction upstairs on the deserted bus that took me home, slowly consuming my Saturday treat, an almost intact Mars Bar, six penn'orth worth of chocolate-covered caramel. So that was her name: *Joan*. Accepting that reality demanded something other than the *Estella* I had imagined for her, it was a disappointment. I had expected something better, more elaborate: *Isault*, perhaps, although I could see why her parents might have hesitated. But at least *Joan* freed me from worship of a straw hat. Because worship surely came into the matter. For weeks now, since the concert debut, my days had been filled with inchoate thoughts of secret passion. All those weeks, Brown the poet had wearied us with schemes to defeat the implacable girl who had summarily rejected his efforts to join the sacred ranks of play-readers. He claimed not to know the name of this vengeful goddess and would barely forgive my knowing, still less forgive the inexplicable truth that she had chosen me without my even asking. On balance, it seemed unkind to tell him and I decided not to; particularly given the far deeper preoccupation that my battered Concise Oxford Dictionary had so far failed to solve. Nearing the end of my Mars Bar and puzzled that fruit seemed fated to play a part in my encounters with girls, I was about to abandon the word *gooseberry* when I spotted the phrase - *to play gooseberry* - set in tiny indented print. *An unwanted third in the presence of two romantically attached.*

One of the two romantically attached arrived home feeling feverish and said he would go and lie down in bed for a while. Mother brought me a cup a tea but went away when I said I had a headache; she would come and talk later when I felt a little better. The sweetness of the Mars Bar seemed almost painfully persistent as I turned over to sleep, thinking of Joan and feeling slightly sick.

*

No longer asleep, that's for sure, although *being sure* is a problem. Staring at the ceiling. There is an awareness of being awake, space delivered to my open eyes as though through a telescope. Everywhere is too bright, too foreign. Surely, space should be attached to knowing where it is, but this telescope space, cluttered with things, fails to complete that trick, it simply *is*, and I know I should say I have no idea where I am, but this strange absence is worse than that, far worse. Knowing there does seem to be *someone* looking at my alien world, but that knowledge comes with the certainly that whoever that someone is, it cannot be me. I have been dispossessed. I have no idea who I am.

Heart racing with fear I manage to lurch myself upright in the bed, aware only of the strangeness of everything in this alien space. Knowledge of what these things are arrives as a kind of proxy, as if rightly belonging to someone else. Not *me*, because I still had no idea who *me* might be. The *I* at the centre of my existence has simply ceased.

The window was the first thing to identify itself. I realised that I knew what it was, and that it was *me* that knew. Gradually, other things pieced themselves together by the act of looking, until I was aware of my room and myself in it. With an inexpressible surge of relief, I find myself blessing the familiarity of my bedroom, reaching out to my remembered past, stitching broken thoughts together, daring to test the limits of what I knew. The smell of cooking and the wireless playing somewhere downstairs seemed to have given me back my life.

I will never know how long I was away. The tea on the bedside table had settled dark brown and stone cold in its cup. I drank it, nonetheless, already seeing it as part of a necessary lie. Not quite sixteen is young for lies like that, although it was a lie that has lived with me for the rest of my life. Holding the cup, I remembered the doctor's sly fishing for signs that Mother may have made a fatal bequest to one or another of her boys. *Did any of us ever swoon? Nothing to worry about, but we should tell him.* Having captured his *epileptic*, how he must have craved for a patient like the boy in Ibsen's *Ghosts*, begging his mother for the sun. Well, unluckily for him, he came asking too soon: he would not capture me with phenobarbital. If I had to lie for my life, then so be it.

That afternoon I fashioned a lie that has served me for seventy years or more. With a certainty born of ignorance, I resolved to avoid whatever it was that precipitated the seizure. The doctor had said Mother would learn to know when she was about to have a turn. I would have to follow suit. The *aura,* he called it: perhaps a persistent taste or smell; or a curious feeling that everything that was happening had already happened before. And here, then, is my secret, a lie I have told for the whole of my life. Not often, but often enough, I have succumbed to Mother's affliction and disappeared from life and if no one ever knew, it was thanks to a curious craving for chocolate or the smell of fresh paint. Really nothing very much.

Mother came to see how I was getting on. I gave her my cup and said I would get up soon; I thought I would go and practise on the organ. She took the cup from my hand: *Oh, you drank it. It must have been cold. I couldn't wake you, you were so asleep.*

Chapter 14

When Mother had gone downstairs, I lay on in bed, reluctant to get up, remembering the fever of first love. Not, I should add, a girl in a straw hat - the object of that innocent first fever had been a boy. His parents had been living abroad and he had joined the school in the middle of the year. A little chap, he seemed perpetually lost, something not helped by his mother (never having received the crucial letter) sending him to school dressed in short trousers. I never knew his name and never addressed a word in his direction, but long naked legs must have stirred some dormant memory of a parade of girls in white snaking past an apprentice to the Electrician's trade. I wondered whether the pleasure secured watching this golden boy each morning stumble into his appointed place was what they meant by love. Because *Love* now was a topic more pressing even than chess.

It was Brown, supremely well-informed on the subject, who spelled out the intricacies of courtship to us, even naming names. He casually declared he had been studying Zeno and had discovered a paradox of his own - the quest for the infinitely elusive, *girl who would*. I attended to his feverish talk largely as looker-on, not daring ask, *would what?* lest he thought me callow. Not for the first time, I regretted I had declined that offer of my Princes End friend. At least, I would have had a foot on the ladder.

To my dismay, my single shy confession about the long-forgotten little boy provoked Bashforth to a storm of denunciation. I was to learn that passion was reserved for girls. *Didn't you see he was a boy?* The distinction seemed unnecessarily subtle to me, but Brown capped it, ominously declaring: *And end up like Lord Montague. Think about that.* In truth, it would have been impossible at the time to think about much else. Newspapers had been filled for days with salaciously ambiguous accounts of this mysterious Montague's fall from grace, Father's *Daily Express* – my only source – disseminating the affair in print almost too large to read. Caught interfering with a group of Boy Scouts, a certain Lord Montague had been arrested and brought to trial. Because Father refused to say, I risked asking Bashforth what the Scouts had been doing that made his interfering such a terrible crime, but he merely shouted, *if you don't know, I'm not saying, but I'll tell you this, you'd better drop the story of that boy.*

Lying that afternoon in unaccustomed indolence, remembering the exchange with the French teacher in the music shop, the realisation I was *romantically attached* arrived as a surge of pure pleasure. If I confessed this to Bashforth it would be unnecessary to add that I had never exchanged a word with Joan - indeed, that we had never met and I had barely seen her face. Joan was not a boy - he would have to be content with that.

A school trip to the *Odeon* cinema that week allowed me to put both face and voice to the object of my passion. I watched the opening scenes of *Romeo and Juliet*, content to weave myself into Shakespeare's all too inadequate account of what might otherwise have been my own romance, with Susan Shentall a pallid imitation of Joan. Unfortunately, the opening scenes were all I managed to see. It took only the Nurse to declare, *his name is Romeo and a Montague*, for the whole cinema to erupt in howls of delighted derision. The name *Montague* is difficult to avoid in that particular play and each occurrence thereafter produced much the same result, howls of, *he's one of them*, drowning out what was left of the dialogue. I hated my fellow men that afternoon. Hated Bashforth, mercilessly poking me in the ribs, baying with the rest. Hated them all for trampling on tender flowers. The thought that Joan herself might have been among those in the balcony above (the cinema being complicit, at the school's request, in this act of heartless segregation) was almost unbearably painful. It sent me home ashamed.

*

I usually made for a side door to get access to the Chapel for my organ practice but on that particular Saturday the big double doors at the top of the steps were slightly open. Drawn by the sound of the organ I went in that way. I had left my copy of Stainer's *The Organ* on the console and someone was playing one of the five practice solos that completed the book. He was making a better job of the piece than I could manage, with one significant qualification – Stainer's carefully annotated pedal notes were missing. The post of Organist in most Methodist Chapels at that time was often filled by pianists from the congregation, willing to do their best. Mr Gittings, the latest to fill the role, was an accomplished musician, but admitted he knew nothing about the organ and could neither select appropriate stops nor play the pedal part. I was, of course, no more than a novice, but I knew enough to spend an enjoyable hour with him that afternoon suggesting registration for the following day's hymns. Our meeting ended with his asking whether I would be willing to sit next to him during the morning service the following day selecting and changing stops and even adding the pedal work to the hymns. The venture was only a partial success and would have come off better without the inevitable clash of legs, but at least the large congregation the following Sunday heard, perhaps for the first time, the massive Open Diapason – a sixteen-foot pipe installed by Messrs Norman & Beard at the dawn of the century, as they were busy building the organ at Lichfield Cathedral.

We fell into the habit of sharing the organ bench, Mr Gittings and I, and as the weeks passed, I graduated from supplementary pedalwork to actually accompanying the congregation in those hymns already familiar to me from my days as an unconfirmed Anglican. It was perhaps inevitable that I would arrive for morning service one Sunday to find a note from Mrs Gittings saying her husband was ill in bed and passing on the message that he knew I'd do my best. As with another premature show of bravura, my organ teacher was mercifully absent - he would have been astonished to hear a selection of far from pious Stourbridge practice pieces put to godly ends as both introit and closing voluntary in the first of what would be very many morning services. As Mr Gittings gratefully withdrew, I inherited his organ console. Although I cannot recall ever being paid or even formally being appointed, while not quite sixteen, I had become a kind of accidental professional organist. I served in that capacity for the next six years.

*

A dog-eared yellow booklet, smelling strongly of old tobacco, arrived a few days later at 160, Leabrook Road inside a large envelope addressed to Mother. As she pulled it out, I saw the sticker on its front - *G.B. Shaw, Arms and the Man. To be Returned* – and felt my pulse rise. She stood reading the letter poked inside, then opened the booklet out, leafing through it in a proprietorial way before handing it to me. *It's your play group. There's to be seven of you, boys and girls. Are you sure you really want to go?* She must have seen the resolution in my face as I clutched my booklet thinking nothing on God's earth would prevent me. *They say you're to play Nicola, I'm not sure your father will be happy with that. You realise you won't know anybody there. Well, not the girls, anyway.* Staring at me I could see she was hoping I would agree. I said that Nicola was a foreign name, and a man not a girl, so that was alright. And that I wanted very much to go.

Adopting Father's prudent approach to punctuality, I arrived at Stourbridge bus station the following Saturday, with at least two hours to spend in draughty reflection on my theatrical debut, perched on a narrow bench with my battered little yellow book and a note inside laconically declaring, *wait until collected.* The station clock had brought me close to despair before the familiar French mistress finally arrived to take me in hand. I walked in her wake for about a mile out of the town along silent streets overhung with lime trees.

A magical sensation of enveloping warmth - my initiation into the wonders of central heating - greeted us at the door of The Pot's house. Heat emanating not from coal fires, still less from paraffin heaters, but simply declaring its luxurious dispersed presence everywhere. The French mistress gestured to a door in the hall, murmuring *Cloak Room* in an oddly conspiratorial fashion, but I shook my head and let The Pot himself usher us into what he called the *Drawing Room*. I had already seen such rooms in countless films, although never imagined I would ever be inside one. *Blythe Spirit* had been the Chapel's Thursday offering that week and for a second it seemed I had somehow walked into Rex Harrison's living room: the same flower-filled garden hazily visible beyond glazed double doors, scattered armchairs dressed in floral chintz, a huge sofa backed against a table crowded with books, a grand piano in the corner, its massive lid decorated with photographs and flowers. There were flowers everywhere.

We were the last to arrive - to discover the cast had already exhausted the supply of places to sit. The French mistress, whom I soon learned to call Frenchie, though not to her face, seemed much at home, fetching the piano stool as her own to sit on. She prodded me down onto a patterned carpet in front of an unlit fireplace filled with logs. The Pot rescued a cigarette from an ashtray he had left to reserve his seat and also settled down to watch - apparently these two were to be our audience.

A girl in the armchair looming over my head leaned down and for a moment I felt the warmth of a face which, on closer examination, was not at all like Susan Shentall. A Stourbridge voice broke the awkward silence in the room with a whispered *you were awfully late, did you get lost?* It was the signal for animated exchanges to break out, although I heard none of them because, incredibly, beneath the general hub-hub the whisper drew excitingly close to my right ear. *I'm Louka. I wangled you Nicola with Frenchie, so say thank you.* I duly mumbled *thank you*, thinking Rex Harrison would have managed it much better. Daring to glance up, she seemed a little annoyed.

The Pot combined his role as audience with that of narrator of Shaw's lengthy Introduction. The character of Nicola does not appear until the second act of *Arms and the Man* and although I had read his lines countless times, it was only on hearing The Pot's description of Nicola's decorated gaiters and wide knickerbockers that it dawned on me that I was supposed to be a middle-aged man. Too late to adjust the voice I had practised, I endured The Pot's complicit chuckle as he looked down at the hunched figure in his fireplace. It was a license for the others to snigger. And they did. Even Joan.

My few lines provided little scope for dazzling theatrical invention and I ended the evening with a sense of anticlimax. It was, of course, only a play, but the apparent relish with which Joan dismissed Nicola with the words: *You were born to be a servant*, rather unnerved me. I heard the piece out to its improbable conclusion, gloomily watching her contrive to marry a boy from The Pot's Sixth Form Classics class. As I struggled to free myself from the crouching posture demanded by my seat in the empty fireplace, Joan reached down and pulled me up, standing very close. Our first conversation was brief and unfortunately shared with her recently-acquired husband who seemed to resent my being there. He was, I think, called Arthur. Joan – who appeared to know him well – explained how it was his turn to arrange the party in the days which followed each meeting of the play-reading group, adding that I would, of course, be coming. Arthur seemed curiously reluctant to confirm this, but she waited long enough to hear a distinctly grudging invitation. Her objective secured, she released my hand with a secret squeeze, patted him on the arm, and walked away. It was an encounter I had rehearsed for weeks and we had barely exchanged ten words. She was gone, pausing only to shake hands with The Pot, and leaving the room bereft. I heard her in the Hall, loftily declaring that her father would be getting impatient waiting in the car.

*

Brown affected a complete lack of interest the following Monday, as I outlined the plot of *Arms and the Man* and described The Pot's impressively heated home, waiting his turn to unleash a searching interrogation on the question of *romantic attachment.* Faced with the question, w*hat's she like, then?* my embarrassed silence served better than anything I might have said and he accepted defeat with enough grace to take it on himself to offer advice on the impending party. We had both seen enough films to accept that cigarettes were an essential element in modern seduction and I readily fell in with his suggestion that I should appear on the scene as an accomplished *smoker.* Two questions only remained: which cigarettes to deploy, and how to obtain them. At first, the solution seemed obvious. I recalled Major Delauney in Paris pulling out a crumpled blue packet of cigarettes, saying they were called *Gitanes* and that Jean-Paul Sartre smoked them. It would have been difficult to improve on this mix of philosophy and French *savoir faire*, but it did not take long to discover that few of the innumerable tobacconists of Stourbridge had even heard of them.

My second line of attack was more allusive, but at least had the merit of English literary associations. In the Science Fourth I had briefly decided to model myself on the Gentleman Cracksman, A.J. Raffles, going so far as to fashion a set of safe-breaking tools from a spool of wire abandoned in Father's shed. It was an infatuation that did not survive the discovery of Lord Peter Wimsey, but I remembered enough of the stories to recall that Raffles smoked "Sullivans" which he kept in a (certainly purloined) silver cigarette case. Since my standing with tobacconists by then had been more or less exhausted, I left it to Brown to make the necessary enquiries. He returned with the news that Sullivan cigarettes had expired along with Raffles himself, adding that the information had cost him a half-packet of Woodbines which he would hold to my account.

It was not until Thursday of that week that the cigarette question was finally solved. The association had never occurred to me before, but I realised that my fellow organist shared his name with the Mr Gittins who kept the little wooden tobacconists shop in Ocker Hill and he confirmed that the old man was, in fact, his father. Tacking as close as I dared to an outright lie, I asked if he could deploy his family connections to secure a suitably exotic cigarette that could be used in a school play. The demand that the offending cigarette would on no account actually be smoked left me with no option but to lie, salving my Methodist conscience with the thought that he could not possibly have believed me. Leaving me sitting at the organ desk he hurried off to catch his father before the shop closed.

The packet of Sobranie "cocktail" cigarettes I acquired later that evening cost me nothing since they were already several years old, having served out their days in a display case. They lasted me three years, albeit unsmoked, apart from two, and were, by any definition, splendidly exotic: ten cigarettes packed flat in a black lacquered box and grouped in pairs, each with a long gold filter tip, they came in five different pastel colours. I made my entrance at Arthur's party two days later in a modest perfumed cloud of pungent smoke from a yellow Sobranie. Possibly because they were so old, the bitter choking taste was almost unbearable, but my consolation was Joan herself, swooping across the room to gather me up, grabbing my smoking hand to demand where the cigarette came from and when she was to be offered one. Those endless magical seconds have lived with me ever since, her hand hovering over the outstretched little lacquered box, hesitating between my own yellow – *now that really would make us a pair* – and a rather fetching lavender. The lavender won, because it matched her frock.

It was only on the journey home, still warm from my theatrical *coup de théâtre*, that a moonstruck boy realised why her choice should have fallen on him. For weeks now, Brown had declared Joan the girl for him, or at the very least for boys like him – battle-hardened sophisticates, schooled in the ways of this or that goddess. Not, it went without saying, for innocents like me. Being a poet, I allowed Brown his *goddess*, acknowledging she was well supplied with worshippers - the permanent attendant shoal of fellow girls warrant enough for that. But he had failed to grasp what suddenly seemed obvious to me on that bus ride home. She had decided, in a word, that I was *safe*.

She confirmed as much on our first true encounter, summoned to the Kardomah coffee shop to meet her one Saturday afternoon some weeks later, before the next play reading. Out of uniform to avoid the school rules and leaning forward to lower her voice, although not quite enough, she brazenly demanded, *have you ever kissed a girl, Alan?* She would never know it had been the intimacy of a name that no one at school used that had me blushing scarlet. She leaned back, declaring she thought as much, adding she liked me, to soften the blow. I made her laugh, she said, and that was good, but mostly because I was uninterested in *all that tiresome stuff*. Perhaps I discovered something that afternoon – all I recall is listening in stunned silence as she mapped out her life. A life that included the "Scholarship" Examinations – territory largely untouched by King Edward's boys (she would, she said, do *well enough*). Thereafter Oxford, where her father had been, and English literature. The play that Saturday was Shaw again: *You Never Can Tell*. I played Philip, twin brother to Joan's flighty Dolly Clandon. I did well enough for Joan in that brotherly style and lasted a good two years as a suitably entertaining boyfriend. Time spent mostly in spirited literary debate. I discovered a great deal, although never that sacred kiss.

Chapter 15

I am in my habitual place in the third row of Assembly seats, Brown at my side murmuring limericks, his latest poetical genre. For some weeks they had begun with *a disconsolate man from Peru*, although the adjective varied, but he now has a new epigraph and is prodding the boys in the row in front to torment me, beating out *a charming young lady called Joan*. I am spared the conclusion as the prefect in the front row springs up to open the door, signal for The Pot's arrival and for the echoing rumble of 400 shuffled feet. It is the last Friday of the year.

The Pot read the Collect for the day, urging us, as he had on the past two hundred days, to be united in one another in pure affection. He would have been pained to discover that we had long since divined what he really meant and considered harping on about *purity* as rather avoiding the point. To the last boy we found the appeal quixotic. To be *united in affection*, however - that was decidedly something different. My head dizzy with thoughts of the unattainable Joan, it was some time before I realised those around me were already singing the morning hymn: *He who would true valour see, let him come hither*. I had once started *Pilgrim's Progress*, although never managed to finish it, but Bunyan's words that day seemed horribly prescient. Bellowing the familiar lie that *no discouragement could make me once lament my first avowed intent to be a pilgrim*, I found myself miserably acknowledging I harboured regrets. Joan had secured the better of our bargain - that much was clear - and the realisation she had known this all the time was reason enough for lament. The Pot could say what he liked about affection but it was not love, and I was in love. Miserably in love. And hearing Mr Bonar at the organ doing his best with Vaughan Williams, I took no pleasure in knowing I could play it better - neither he, nor Joan, nor anyone else, would ever know. There was a bitter price to pay for living a double life.

The rest of that Assembly was taken with successes of the year, the finale a procession of The Pot's favoured children, classical scholars in the main, translated into Big Boys, prefects for the next two years. Lumbering across the stage to receive their cap badge, precious emblem of their rank, they were mercifully unaware of Brown's poetic commentary – a limerick of gothic proportions, spoiled only by the occasional weak rhyme. We were dismissed with the stern reminder that Saturday was a school day and that The Pot himself would attend to note unwonted absences.

As we filed out, a master was standing under the final arch of the little colonnade at the side of the Hall, someone I didn't know, apart from the fact that he taught Latin. He seemed to single me out as I snaked by with the others, calling: *I know you have a way to come, Kennedy, but you'll not forget absences will be recorded tomorrow, will you?* When I looked back, he was still standing there, apparently waiting for someone.

My journey to school the following morning was much concerned with Major Delauney. That enigmatic injunction from a master I barely knew had served only to reinforce a persistent vague anxiety that had consumed me ever since my Great Deception. It seemed utterly impossible, but if anyone was going to discover my guilty secret, it would be Major Delauney. God alone knew exactly how, but I was convinced he had deployed his skills in espionage to discover the secret of my O level French results and I stood on the threshold of ignominious exposure, perhaps even expulsion. I should explain I had made virtually no progress in French after three years of Major Delauney's instruction. To say that he was an ineffectual teacher is to imply he committed some minimal level of application to the task. This was not so: we learned a great deal from Major Delauney, but this did not include instruction in the French language. He left his colleagues to do the best they could with the untutored consequences of the many enjoyable hours we had spent in his benevolent company. Like all other subjects, the O level examination in French had been preceded by a "mock" version and my performance had been so spectacularly inadequate that failure in the examination proper was a racing certainty.

And so it would have been, had I not met Elizabeth, my raspberry cane neighbour, the evening following the O level examination in English literature. As we stood at the garden gate, commiserating over the vicissitudes of the scholar's life, I asked how she had got on in the English paper that day. To learn that she was to take English tomorrow. Her school, like mine, was located also in another county and followed a different examination timetable. In fact, her trial of the day had been French and she offered me a rather crumpled examination paper to look at, saying I could use it as practice if I liked.

In fact, the examination I was presented with the following afternoon was not *similar* to the one Miss Furnivall lent me – it was *identical*. A coincidence that had been judged too unlikely to matter, delivered me a pass in O level French. Even – an astonished Mr Lucy said – a very creditable pass, although I blushed at his words.

I sat on the bus to school that morning my stomach hollow with the conviction it would be my last journey. Plainly, I was to be exposed, although exactly *how* Major Delauney had uncovered the deception defeated me. It could not have been from Elizabeth herself – she had already confessed that the English examination paper I had given her had been the one she had taken on the following day: she was far too fearful ever to reveal the truth.

*

Only masters who had classes to take presented themselves for the final Assembly of the year, and the rows of professional spectators behind The Pot were a little thinner than usual, but I took no comfort in the fact that Major Delauney was not there. Probably he was already waiting in The Pot's room beyond the fateful green door. A prefect read the scripture of the day. Matthew chapter 5 was a favourite of the Minister at Ocker Hill, but the familiar words: *Let your light so shine before men that they may see your good works,* seemed cruelly imbued with unsuspected meaning. The reading over, The Pot rose to speak, but I saw already how easily he could put the words to work, shining the light of truth, eliding from good works to bad.

Barely listening, I was busy composing his fatal speech until, that is, Brown prodded me to get up. The Pot was still speaking. I heard him explain how my name had somehow been missed, but here was the remedy: if Kennedy, R., late of the Fifth Science, would stir himself, here was his prefect's badge.

The Pot shook my hand when I reached the stage, apparently disconcerted by applause more enthusiastic than the event warranted, murmuring, *you seem a popular chap*. Remembering the reception we gave the irate Director at the Lycée Lakanal, I could have explained they were clapping for want of anything better to do and it had little to do with me, but he would have thought me boastful. I returned to my seat in a state as close to bliss as God allowed.

That same enigmatic Latin master was waiting in the colonnade outside. He had been talking to Mr Bonar and, as he saw me, stepped across to shake my hand, muttering something in Latin he clearly believed I understood. Beyond him, Mr Bonar was watching the two of us. As I caught his eyes he looked away, his face betraying an expression he seemed at pains to hide, almost a smile.

*

The prefects' room was a basement under the stage of the Assembly Hall, with windows which would have overlooked the playground had not their position, set high along one wall, demanded something to stand on to see anything at all. I made my entrance after a truncated chemistry lesson. Bashforth and Brown came with me a little of the way, standing wistfully at a distance as I knocked the door. My Prefectorial induction did not take long, comprising little more than a handshake with the Head Boy. He was repeating his Scholarship examinations and had little time for anything else, spending his days in solitary subterranean revision. Rarely seen about the school, I had always taken him to be one of the masters. Sporting a luxuriant blond moustache, he must have been almost twenty, squeezed absurdly into a tiny desk. It was difficult to imagine he ever wore the battered school cap dangling from the back of his chair.

He stood up when I told him my name, towering over me. *I've heard about you – you must be the Late Extra*. He saw my puzzled face and explained how a deputation of boys had secured my unwonted elevation. They had pleaded my cause with one of the masters, pressing on him as a mark of my peculiar merit the fact I lived so far away, what's more, in a place so inaccessibly remote that no one had heard of it. Despite this topographical burden, my commitment to extracurricular attachments of one flavour or another meant I virtually lived in the school. I can only assume the master petitioned The Pot on my behalf. Fraudulently, of course, because those well-meaning boys could hardly have elaborated on the only attachment of significance in my life.

All through this recital he had been glancing impatiently at his neglected books. Squeezing himself back into his desk I realised I had been dismissed. As I reached the door he called after me: *You won't get anywhere with her, you know.* Possibly it was the thought of that deputation, but I found myself possessed, however briefly, of the confidence to say, *I know that.* Hearing my own voice I scarcely dared turn round, but he was already busy scribbling notes in a book. I had imagined Bashforth at least would be waiting for me, but neither of them were there.

*

That Sunday I found the Minister waiting for me on the Chapel steps after the morning service. He had been invited to take a mid-day meal with a member of the congregation, something she arranged every year in memory of her Father who died on this particular day. She always invited the organist and since I had apparently taken Mr Gittins' place, he was sure I would be welcome to join them. It was not far and would not be out of my way. I walked with him down Spring Street and turned into Toll End Road passing the curtained windows of a row of tiny terraced houses. He seemed to know the way, suddenly disappearing into a narrow cleft between the buildings. The alleyway led to a communal back yard: on one side, six identical scrubbed stone steps; on the other, a row of six pierced wooden doors ranged like the lavatories of St Mark's Primary School. A wall at the far end enclosed this minute patch of Ocker Hill that had changed little since the 1850s.

The Minister was allocated one of the two chairs in a room that otherwise had little else but a sink, a gas stove and a television set. We were to know that Mildred had examinations tomorrow. She was at the Grammar School in Tipton, her mother said, and needed the front room to study. We would have to make do where we were. Since she refused to sit, standing erect by the gas cooker, we stood in an awkward group eyeing the vacant chair until she declared the organist must have it *while he has his cup of tea*, adding, to avoid any uncertainty on the matter, *because he won't be staying.*

Mildred's manifestly reluctant father was called down from an upstairs room and pressed to deliver my tea. It arrived in a wide porcelain teacup decorated in a startling floral design that would have been familiar to Miss Eliza Bennett. Ocker Hill must have boasted hundreds of similar wedding presents, living out their precious unused days in cupboards. Perhaps because my particular cup was so fragile or because I had inevitably sunk deep into the upholstery of my chair, he seemed to have difficulty handing it me, waiting nervously until I had an adequate grip on the saucer. No one spoke. I was conscious only of silent scrutiny, three sets of eyes waiting until I had finished this necessary preliminary to my rapid departure.

God alone knows how it came about. I lifted my cup and as milky tea first touched my lips, I found myself holding no more than a single delicately decorated handle. Slowly but inexorably the cup was detaching itself, stringy fibres of glue stretching out across a widening gap, finally precipitating scalding pain about my lap. It must have been my howl that brought the third character onto the scene. I had managed to stand and by adopting a kind of hopping kangaroo gait, tugging all the while at the belt of my trousers for relief, had brought myself to the door of the front room, when it opened. A girl in school uniform looked past me into the room, cooly asking what all the noise was about.

The initial suggestion, enthusiastically endorsed by the Minister, was to kit me out in trousers fetched from a wardrobe in the room above, allowing my own to be taken to the dry cleaners tomorrow. Mildred's father, who was plainly several sizes larger than me, had fled upstairs in search of trousers before I had had time to protest that I would prefer to go home as I was, since the pain had subsided. I would explain to Mother how the accident had come about. In that case, Mildred must certainly go with me. To return with the damaged trousers, her mother said, although clearly she had in mind the need for a witness to whatever account I might give of life in Toll End Road. I knew that Mother would never agree, but it seemed pointless to explain.

I heard the saga of the broken cup from Mildred as we walked as far as 160, Leabrook Road. Rearranging his wife's treasured collection of cups to make room for something else, her father had managed to break a handle off. Fearful of the inevitable retribution, he had effected a repair with the only tube of glue to hand. Mildred's glue, in fact - something left over from a long-forgotten school project. The repair looked well enough and since the cups were never used, the deception comfortably outlived any recollection of carrying it out. Until, that is, the unexpected arrival of the organist that Sunday had called for an extra cup. Mildred's expression suggested the affair was, then, largely my fault. It was my first insight into the mind of this new person in my life.

Chapter 16

Mother listened to my story about the broken cup in silence, simply telling Ian to, *look through the front window and see whether that girl's still there*. He waited until she went away. Mildred never spoke of it again to me. It seemed, however, that I had inadvertently secured yet another girl friend. Throughout that hot summer holiday, it was a rare Sunday now when I would not find Mildred after the morning service seated with those who had stayed to hear the voluntary. Not exactly waiting, more companionably willing to walk with me a little. We were only strolling side by side and certainly not *walking out*. And if we somehow contrived to miss the watching eyes of Leabrook Road, I persuaded myself it was only because there were more convenient routes to take.

I decided that to mention Joan to someone I barely knew would be a kind of betrayal and Mildred never asked whether I had some particular girl of my own. Since a moonstruck boy is easy enough to diagnose, I suspect she guessed and kept her peace, accepting to walk three abreast until I came to my senses. Perhaps she was relieved that I never asked whether she had a boy of her own – I will never know.

These morning July walks became a habit, the paths we took soon becoming our own invariable familiar way, winding between the abandoned mine shafts of Ocker Hill, transformed now to tiny lakes, alive with fish. Gangs of giggling boys in search of Sunday lovers would sometimes stalk us, hiding behind cliffs of purple willowherb to watch, but since we were not lovers, they soon went looking for more promising prey.

*

I am sitting in the Kardomah Café in Stourbridge High Street, opposite Gwendolen Fairfax putting on a show for customers at neighbouring tables. It is Saturday, and later this evening The Pot will host the first play reading of a new school year: *The Importance of Being Earnest* with Joan as an energetic Gwendolen, a leading part. My own little yellow book had arrived with a scribbled note inside from Frenchie: *Dr Chasuble, please.* At least I had some lines to speak, although none that I could find were addressed to Gwendolen.

Joan had been listening to the recital of my proposed diet of A level physics, chemistry and mathematics with an expression approaching disbelief. It was bad enough, she said, that *anyone* would waste their life on all that stuff but why would *I,* of all people, chose such a thing? Couldn't I see it would be the ruin of me? Had I not worked out what that prefect business was really all about? She had gone very red, her chest heaving, suddenly blurting out, *you know I don't mean you. I mean the likes of you. God, can't you see?*

Aware of what she was trying to say I saw myself – possibly for the first time – truly through someone else's eyes. Self-possessed to a fault, I had never been conscious of the yawning chasm that separated the likes of me from Joan. I saw her watching her quaint boy as you might examine an exotic creature collected on some visit to a cannibal island, something she'd daringly decided to cage. Had I not realised, she said, how The Pot resented the boys foisted on his school? My sort of boy. Had I not noticed how rarely boys like me got into his precious class in Ancient History and Greek? If I let The Pot get his way, all I'd get was scraps – things tossed for the hairy-footed to eat. She would not have let him get away with that.

It was no use asking what she meant. I knew perfectly well what she meant. I may believe I lived in two worlds, but carrying Ocker Hill on my back I would never properly live in either. I hated Joan in that moment more, I think, than ever I had hated anyone. Hated her for her effortless disdain. Hated that she knew things it was now too late for me to know. Hated this elegant creature, strangely now no longer a girl, dressed in that curiously careless style purchased with something more complicated than money. And thinking of Mildred's dress, bulging with petticoats – the one she called her *best* - I felt myself flush with shame. I hated Joan in that instant for owning my soul. For knowing I could not bear the thought she might ever let me go.

She changed the subject, taking refuge in poetry, saying we shouldn't squabble and she had a question for me. Her Examination Board gave her a choice. A lot depended on which way you jump with a thing like that. Chaucer or Milton? - she wasn't sure. *What did I think of Milton?* The question was a peace offering - meek inquiring eyes suddenly holding mine, allowing her avid audience to imagine I could frame a sensible reply. I heard myself stammer out the half-remembered residue of the most recent walk with Mildred. *Don't you have Gerard Manley Hopkins? Isn't he a choice as well?*

The neighbouring heads looked up, startled, as Joan exploded, *Oh, my God - Ken's found himself a girl. I'm right, aren't I? Come on, what's she like?* Seeing my stricken face, she composed herself, suddenly serious. *No, honestly, tell her from me you're best to stay away from anything after 1850. She'll thank me for it.* She ignored my feeble protest that there really wasn't a *she*, speaking almost to herself. *I know I'm right. Not Gerard Manley Hopkins. Anyway, he's not, is he? Manly, I mean? Dappled this and dappled that – it's creepy.*

Dr Chasuble was no more than a modest success that night. The Pot acknowledged my efforts at Wilde's laboured wit, but Joan had made me see condescension in his complacent smiles, something not altogether kind. Even his customary comment as I left with Frenchie, *you're in good time for your bus, Kennedy,* seemed somehow demeaning.

*

I went in search of Mr Eliot the following Monday. He taught senior boys English in the school and would surely sympathise with a proposition – not yet even shared with Mother - that had seemed so obvious when it occurred to me that I had flushed with relief. I would drop one of my science subjects and take instead the A level examination in English literature? Joan had taught me to look it squarely in the face: taught me that what she wanted, I wanted too. Mr Eliot could not recall that he had once complemented me on an essay in an English class some years before. Indeed, although he was kind enough, it was obvious he had no idea who I was. He took it on himself to explain that A level subjects did not exist in isolation. Even if it *were* possible (pursing his lips to underline the hypothetical), I would have to study History alongside it to have any chance of success. And a foreign language – had I thought of that? In any case, there was a timetable. It would be impossible to substitute English literature for any of my science subjects – the idea was absurd. *You're not the first to have second thoughts, Kennedy. They fade when you find your feet.* And with that I was sent on my way. He had, at least, remembered my name.

*

The first chess match of the new term was against a large Public School. It was our first encounter. Although I had played as third board in the previous year, TELC made the tactical decision that I should play the bottom board. It would secure us at least one near-certain win and allow him to deploy his secret weapon, a "thirteen-plus" boy who had come from a Steiner School and was apparently very strong. The game was scheduled for Saturday afternoon, a coach setting off from the school yard immediately after classes, leaving no time to eat. We arrived, weary and bedraggled after a long journey and liberally decorated with the remains of the sandwiches eaten en route. To be met by a boy, immaculately dressed, as for a funeral, in severe black apart from an alarmingly striped tie. He led us in silence down a long corridor and left us standing at the open door of what must have been a prefects' room while he went inside, although not before snatching a paper that had been pinned to the door and letting it fall to the floor.

Bashforth daringly stepped across the threshold and we straggled after him, to confront a scene evidently contrived for our benefit. Boys dressed in immaculate black, apart from matching striped ties, had ranged themselves about the panelled room in a style familiar from the works of Lord Dunsaney, lounging in leather chairs behind newspapers or posed in artificial little groups deep in unconvincing conversation. A pall of blue smoke filled the air. The boy who had led us here was apparently in dispute with a group at the other end of the room and showed no sign of rejoining us.

I picked up the crumpled paper and straightened it out. It read NO OIKS or, possibly, NOOIKS. Bashforth took it from me. Upside down, it looked vaguely Russian, but was no less indecipherable. He bent down and carefully returned it to the floor, whispering, *what's oiks?* I never got the chance to say that I had no idea, because our guide reappeared to offer the unnecessary apology that we would not be playing here, but somewhere else. We followed him further down the corridor and into a room painted in startling white. Glass-fronted cabinets along the walls, together with packets of bandage on a steel table, declared the place to be some kind of infirmary. Tables with chess boards and clocks had been arranged down the middle of the room following the line of a broad red stripe on the floor (we were never to learn the purpose of this stripe).

My bottom board opponent had yet to arrive. Someone was sent to coax him from whatever occupation was apparently more engaging than chess, while I sat at my desk straightening the polished Staunton pieces on the board in front of me. They looked brand new. Bashforth stooped over me brandishing a battered dictionary plucked from his satchel and smelling strongly of the cheese and pickle sandwiches he was keeping for the journey home. He was pointing: *Oik – An uncouth man, possibly onomatopoeic in imitation of uncultivated speech.*

*

My memory of that fateful game of chess comes, even now, seething with the indignity of *oik*; that, and the antiseptic scent of the room. I had barely noticed my opponent arrive. Much older than I had expected and taller than me, he was also dressed in the severe mourning that seemed to serve these boys as uniform. His grasp of the game put me in mind of Father's brief flirtation with chess. That is, he knew virtually nothing beyond how the pieces moved and, even then, was sufficiently uncertain about what to do with his two Knights that he left them rooted to their home squares until I captured them. In truth, there was little else to do in that game but capture his pieces. and his response to my unambitious Ruy Lopez opening had been to advance pawns doggedly across the board in a progressively pointless blockade. He clung to this fatal strategy until its inevitable collapse, managing to lose, in spectacular succession, his queen, a bishop, two pawns, and eventually, yet another unprotected bishop. To my surprise, he seemed blithely unconscious of the scale of the disaster that had befallen him. Rather than resign, he continued negligently pushing his dwindling forces into an increasingly hopeless position until no more than three or four remained. I was suddenly aware he was simply toying with me: that he considered both the game and his opponent of no consequence and that he had better things to do with his time. I determined on revenge. Rather than checkmate him, I would first remove all of his remaining pieces. It proved more difficult than I had imagined to avoid checkmating him, but I persisted, and our bizarre game of all against none ran on into the afternoon. It took the combined forces of the two adjudicators to bring it to an end, the win sealing a four-two victory for the school.

*

TELC dismissed Bashforth to the rear of the coach, securing the seat next to mine for the return journey. He proceeded to deliver a lecture to the world at large on the nature of gentlemanly conduct: How many times had he explained that chess was more than a game? … if Kennedy could not play in a more honourable fashion, he should count himself lucky to remain in the team … after Kennedy's prolonged humiliation of his opponent, the team may not be invited to play a return match … surely Kennedy knew that if you are much the stronger player it is your duty to offer your opponent the opportunity to have the game adjudicated, not to demean him. It went on for so long that Bashforth had succeeded in advancing far enough up the aisle to emit a squeak of protest - brutally overtaken by a demand that Kennedy write a letter of apology. TELC himself would approve the letter on Monday morning.

Aware that the real affront had been our opponents' in presenting someone as a member of their team who cared nothing for the game, the journey continued in an atmosphere of sullen mutiny. If anyone had been humiliated in my absurd game it had been the miserable oik deemed too uncivilised to deserve anything better. How could

132

TELC not know that? The seeds of rebellion were planted in my breast that afternoon; I determined that no power on earth would make me apologise. If the price I must pay was exclusion, then so be it - he could whistle for his letter. That was not, however, the reason it was never written.

Chapter 17

I recall feeling hot on that coach-ride back to school, an odd feverish state that persisted when I eventually caught the bus to Ocker Hill. There was a long wait at Dudley while a new driver was installed. I sat in my habitual place on the upper deck staring idly down into the street, suddenly aware that every attempt to swallow provoked a sharp stab of pain down one side of my throat. Not that I had anything particular to swallow, my thermos flask had been long since emptied. By the time I staggered off the bus and made my way down Leabrook Road, I had a raging thirst and the pain had spread to both sides of my throat.

Mother was cooking something in the kitchen and I managed to croak that I seemed to have caught a cold and would go and lie down, that I didn't feel like eating anything but was dreadfully thirsty. She called after me that she would bring me a cup of tea. I reached my bed overwhelmed by the awareness of the onset of a seizure - my first in many months – relief flooding my mind that I had managed to reach safety just in time. It was many years before I learned that it is a constituent property of this mysterious aura to be, invariably, *just in time*. That is, I presume, its function.

∗

Have you any ice cream? We can try him with that. Mother must have brought the tea, but it was not Mother's voice. My heart racing at the thought the doctor had been called, that I had been discovered too deeply asleep to wake. It was Dr Hildebrand talking about ice cream, leaning over me in the bed, pressing something like a cold metal spoon against my tongue, shining a tiny torch into my throat. The bedroom was inexplicably dark, just the little light on at the side of the bed. I must have been unconscious for hours.

Dr Hildebrand kept a practice in Wednesbury on the ground floor of some disused municipal building. I recall a large waiting area set out with benches facing the door to a single consulting room. I had not been there often, but my recollection was that the place was invariably packed, mostly mothers shuffling children in a slow progression along the benches to the periodic summons, in a strong guttural German accent, *Next patient, please.*

Before she fled her native land as a refugee, Dr Hildebrand must have acquired holy orders in some sufficiently impressive nonconformist doctrine to be invited to deliver sermons at Chapels throughout the region. She was apparently a celebrated theologian, although the Ocker Hill congregation, largely innocent of theology, greatly preferred our own Minister's, much shorter, offerings. On days when she came to preach, she did not sit with the congregation before the sermon, preferring to wait in the vestry. She was present when the Minister went through the hymns with me, deciding which verses to omit, but she took no part in the deliberations, quietly sitting in the corner, waiting her turn. Albeit a gentle, self-effacing, godly woman, Mother's hysterical complaint that the State had foisted a German doctor on her family must have infected my fevered mind: while she merely disliked Dr Hildebrand, I grew up fearing her. Indeed, many of my childhood nightmares, particularly those born of fever, were of Dr Hildebrand - menacingly prowling the house in search of inadequately hidden infant prey. Mercifully unaware of her homicidal reputation, this was the woman who had willingly abandoned her bed in the middle of night to carry me through the front door of 160, Leabrook Road, wrapped in a coarse red blanket that was not my own, out into the smell of cold street air and into the waiting ambulance. I remember Father calling after her that there was no ice cream and thinking this was a funny thing to say. Mother tried to climb into the ambulance with me, but the men held her back while they closed the doors.

The first two days of my three weeks in Hospital were spent settling on a name for my illness. The matron had discovered Stuart was a medical student and for reasons I never quite fathomed this information translated itself into an unusual level of concern. Given Dr Hildebrand's initial diagnosis of *diphtheria*, my case had been treated as an emergency and would have had serious consequences, not the least being to define the school chess team, if not the whole school, as contacts to be traced and possibly quarantined. A tall man appeared later that morning to stand at the foot of my bed and talk about me to the nurse. I was told he was a *Consultant* from the hospital in Wolverhampton – his status confirmed by the fact he wore normal clothing - apart from a stethoscope - and was addressed by the nurses, somewhat perversely, as "Mr". It needed only the most perfunctory examination for him to dismiss *diphtheria*. I was, he declared, suffering from *Quinsy*. I had never heard this word, which seemed almost too dainty to be any kind of disease, but it, too, was abandoned in the following days, in favour of the more mundane *Tonsillitis*. I got the impression he was disappointed. In any case, since the only treatment available for all three complaints was the administration of massive doses of penicillin, I had already been committed to the mercy of *fever nurses* armed with nightmarish hypodermic syringes. The cure for whatever was afflicting me, albeit very painful, was miraculously rapid, easily outpacing the diagnosis.

The *Fever Van*, as they called it in Ocker Hill, had brought me to Moxley Isolation Hospital, a cluster of buildings set in extensive wooded grounds on the outskirts of Wednesbury. Bounded on three sides by high walls and on the fourth by the Walsall canal it was home to the victims of every imaginable virulent infection. As I recovered enough to notice, I discovered that among my immediate neighbours were patients with measles, polio, typhoid fever, whooping cough, and tuberculosis; cholera was not unknown in Moxley; even leprosy, although the nurses admitted that was unusual. The governing principle of this temple to the *Germ Theory* of disease was a policy of severe social exclusion, ruthlessly applied. The only healthy inhabitants were the medical staff, who apparently survived by excluding all others. Visitors – even close relatives - to what was, in effect, a kind of benign prison were, without any exception, forbidden.

Since my recovery had been relatively rapid, I spent most of my three weeks in the hospital wondering why I was there. The nurses declared I could not leave because I was dangerously under-weight, christening me *The Belsen Boy*, but although there was some truth in this tasteless jibe, nothing at all was done to remedy the matter – there was little hope of growing fat on a catering regime that had changed little since the depths of war. It was only as I was about to be discharged that I discovered the true reason for my detention. The Consultant who listened to my heart on the day of my admission claimed to have detected a "murmur". He returned thereafter on an almost daily basis to listen again, finally asking me to confirm that my brothers had also been born with fused toes on both feet. The question seemed so inconsequential I mumbled that, so far as I knew, they had; it was, however, only two toes, not all of them, and this very modest deformity was, in any case, barely visible. I was self-conscious about my toes, the nurses already teasing me as web-footed, and I rather resented this haughty Mr raising the matter. He must have realised I had taken offence, because he told me to ask my brother the medical student, whether he thought this might portend, however slightly, some kind of neural tube defect? How could I have known then, how prescient this observation was? He had almost certainly detected the anomaly in my aortic valve which had developed a bicuspid, rather than the normal tricuspid, form. But if I ever relayed this mysterious question to Stuart, I have no recollection of his reply.

I was soon able to get out of bed and pass my time more or less as I pleased, even, on warmer days, wandering through the grounds, clad in the hospital's bright green outdoor pyjamas, ill-fitting garments sufficiently peculiar to identify me should I decide on escape. There was nothing to read, apart from an edition of *The Works of William Shakespeare*, freely available from the hospital library – a dusty bookcase housing, in the main, abandoned comic books. This battered relic was printed (so it declared) on "War Economy" paper, so thin that words from both sides of each page sometimes aligned themselves to form weird amalgams. It did, however, permit me to read *The Winter's Tale*, a play sanctified by the knowledge that Joan had declared it to be one of her A level set texts.

Apart from *Romeo and Juliet*, in an edition I realised must have been pruned to the needs of twelve-year-olds, I had read nothing by Shakespeare. *The Winter's Tale* proved a challenge. There was no Introduction and although there were footnotes, these were no more than cryptic circular references to even more plays I had yet to read. It was only the thought that I was in some obscure way keeping step with Joan that kept me going, but I was soon plagued by doubts. In particular, the ambition to renounce science for the world of letters seemed reckless given the discovery that Shakespeare wrote in a language I barely recognised as English. Even if I deciphered *The Winter's Tale* to its end – and my rate of progress suggested I might need a disease more severe than tonsillitis to do so – there were dozens of other plays. In any case, what exactly would I learn from reading it? Quadratic equations were tiresome, but at least they led to particular answers. If *The Winter's Tale* was going to be the answer, what exactly had been the question?

Consoled by the thought that my own unattainable Perdita would by now be facing these same uncertainties in her far-off Stourbridge school, I persisted to the triumphal end, sitting high in my hospital bed, the dusty book heavy on my lap. I remember Hermione's restoration at the end brought me close to tears, although she would hardly have recognised the silent pronunciation I had assigned to her alien name. But I cried I think, more for Mother's unhappy state than for Hermione's, marvelling at the twist of coincidence that had brought me to this strange play about the insane fury of jealous love.

*

Father fetched me home in the Austin Big Six, waiting for me at the foot of the steps to the hospital entrance. It was raining, but that was as close as he was allowed. He helped me into the front seat of the car, doing his best to sound cheerful with, *we'll soon get that smell off you*, winding the window down despite the rain. As we moved off, he seemed to remember we had not been on speaking terms when they'd taken me away, managing only a few stilted questions about my hospital days. I struggled to reply. The truth was I barely knew who he was. I had been so long away I would not have been surprised to find him with a monstrous grizzled beard like the Count of Monte Cristo. Eventually, I remembered to ask him why Mother wasn't with him, but *you'll see what's what when we get home*, left me none the wiser. At 160, Leabrook Road, he said he would go and put the car away, leaving me to go inside. Mother was not there to greet me. The dresser in the kitchen had been folded up, although she never left it like that - it gave the place an abandoned air.

Stuart was in the living room. He had brought a pile of books downstairs and installed himself in Father's chair. There were too many things on his lap to get up, but he seemed pleased to see me, saying he had been sure at the time that it wasn't diphtheria. It was not the first time I had heard him try this special doctor's voice, but I felt my heart-rate rise, wondering why he looked so nervous. It must be bad news if he was so unwilling to talk about it. Had Mother been taken ill again? Perhaps she was in hospital. Perhaps she was dead – was that what he was trying so earnestly not to say? He saw me glance at the door and said: *She's gone to visit Aunt Bessie*. Then he said I should sit down because he wanted to tell me something.

Mother had had a seizure the day I had been taken away. It was in the afternoon and was so bad she had bitten her tongue. Father had sent for the doctor, but she wouldn't have Dr Hildebrand, and a doctor from Wolverhampton had to come. This new doctor had come to see her several times since. She had a new medicine now. The seizures had stopped but her *melancholia* was much worse. Stuart stopped at this point, saying he knew what I was going to say, but nobody was going to do ECT again. The doctor from Wolverhampton had suggested something completely different. A new treatment for depression that worked so well it was almost a miracle. He pointed to his right eye, running his finger back and forth underneath the eyebrow: *Just here. An incision lets you reach the affected part. A tiny incision – and it doesn't hurt. She might even come home the same day.*

Father had been so long putting the car away I realised he had wanted Stuart to explain this new treatment for Mother. He must have believed that Stuart, being almost a doctor, would put it in words I would understand, would make me see there was nothing else to be done – the operation was all that was left. But Stuart knew that his voice betrayed his words – he had stopped looking at me. Stuart could never tell lies. None of us could. As I went upstairs, he called after me: *Talk to her, she'll listen to you.*

*

I went upstairs and lay down on the bed. The room had been tidied up, almost as if I might not be coming back. The sheets were stretched tight like in a hospital. The pillow wasn't there. I knew Mother must have put it in the wardrobe, but I could not summon the energy to look for it. More than anything at that moment I wanted to be somewhere else: back in my own bed in the hospital, back even in the Lycée dormitory; *anywhere*, so long as it was away from Mother's malaise and the horror of this latest cure. It was cowardly, but I prayed for an end to endless hopes of a cure; an end to having to take sides. Poor Stuart – forced to argue Father's case when he did not believe a word of it. He knew I would never tell Mother that *incisions*, however small, would cut misery out. Wrapped in clever words it was just another kind of witchcraft. Unhappiness was not made of something you could cut - even a schoolboy could see that. I remembered the way Father had looked on that Guy Fawkes night when Alastair had come with his bucket of fireworks. Father surely knew the ECT had been a mistake so dreadful he would never acknowledge the harm it had done. It was why he had not wanted to come home that night, why he had stayed to look after the fire. It was the same now. He had been half an hour putting the car away.

Chapter 18

It was very late when Mr Jencks brought Mother back in Auntie Bessie's car. Father had gone to bed because he had to go to work tomorrow, but he let me sit by the fire to wait. When I heard the car, I went into the kitchen and stood waiting for the door to open. Mother paused for a moment in the doorway when she saw me, then asked whether I'd had anything to eat. Ian was with her and she told me to put the kettle on while she got him to bed. He looked almost asleep already. He grinned and said, *I knew you were coming back today.*

Thinking of *The Winter's Tale*, I had imagined Mother would cry when she saw me, hold me close, hug me, perhaps even kiss me, although she knew I hated that. But apart from seeming a little irritated that Father – as ever - had closed the dresser door, she seemed not unhinged at all; and he was always forgetting about the dresser door. It was as if I had never been away. If there was theatre in the attitude she struck, one hand resting on the door, it was as far from Shakespeare as you can imagine. Stuart had braced me to expect someone too far in thrall to misery even to welcome me, and we both had seen her hag-ridden like that often enough. But the Mother who placidly greeted me that night was as she always had been in the best of times. And if that was pretence, I can only guess the price she paid to achieve it.

The following morning, Father explained that Mother would be going away with Auntie Bessie at the end of the week to stay at a Health Farm in Malvern. I had no idea why she would want to go to a farm, it seemed ridiculous, but he said it had nothing to do with farming, it was more like a kind of hotel. There were mineral water springs in Malvern and special places where you drink the water or even bathe in it. They were going to one of these places. Mother explained how Uncle Leslie had gone to a spa in Malvern every year and that was why Auntie Bessie had suggested it. Father laughed and said, *and a fat lot of good it did him*, but she said nothing, doing her best to keep the peace. It seemed I was watching the burnt-out remains of some ferocious dispute, fought while I was in hospital: Father and Stuart ranged against the two intransigent sisters. But however weak Mother's case against the miraculous *small incision* might have been, it seemed she had won and her prize was, yet again, at least a temporary escape. Father grumbled that it was stupid to go all that way just to drink water and eat carrots, turning aside with, *isn't that right, Stuart?* but Stuart said nothing. His heart was no longer in it and he laughed when Mother said she could bring some carrots back if we liked.

*

The Sunday morning that Mother left for Malvern I was uncertain whether I should wait with her until Auntie Bessie came or set off for the Chapel morning service (and discover whether some unknown other had been found to play the organ). Mother settled the matter, telling Ian to go and find something to do outside, her voice so charged with anxious intent that he scuttled away without protest. She wanted me on my own, she said, because I would be sixteen while she was away. *Did I know sixteen was a special birthday?* Barely waiting for a reply, she said she had decided to give me my present now and not leave it until she returned.

Of course, the boys at school knew what was special about sixteen - some of them talked of little else - but I could only guess how Mother had come by this secret. Sixteen, as Brown was fond of observing, was when you *could*. He had written poems on the subject. Even Joan – and this was not so very long ago - had leaned back in her Kardomah seat one Saturday, airily declaring, *I'm sixteen now, did I tell you?* I have never forgotten her laughing at my startled face as she added, a*nd if you want to know, I am thinking about it, although Mother says better not. Mind you, young Arthur's always saying he wants my virgin heart.* I spent the bus ride home from The Pot's that night, tormented by the fateful word *always*, my thoughts consumed with sad reflections on a life not lived; I cannot remember the play we read.

Mother had handed me an envelope and told me to open it, taking pleasure in my awestruck expression. Three magnificent five-pound notes: huge white crinkly things, black with printer's ink, almost too big to be money. I realise now she said so little because she dared not claim to know me well enough to say *better not* – mothers like that being only found in Stourbridge. What she did say, however, was the closest either of my parents ever came to offering instruction in the mysteries of sex. Instruction so mysterious in Mother's case that it was many a year before I realised what she meant. Her words were awkwardly blurted out: *There. You can buy the things you need yourself, and mind you do. You'll be careful, won't you? Ask your brother if you're not sure.*

If Mother believed I took the sense of what she meant – that my sixteen-year-old thoughts would naturally turn to the purchase of contraceptive rubber goods – she was certainly mistaken. Ecstatic thoughts of quite a different kind raced so far ahead of anything she said, I barely heard. I could buy the mirrored box from my catalogue of conjuring tricks; and the shabby little shop in Great Bridge, not far from the station, had piles of organ music, not expensive at all for someone with fifteen pounds. A solitary triode valve housed in what was left of a battered metal frame painted dull green and stamped *Marconi* had already joined the crystal set in my bedroom. It had the personal guarantee of the insalubrious keeper of these relics of forgotten combat that it lacked only a battery to make it work. With riches on this miraculous scale the single high-tension battery in the window of his War Surplus Store in Wednesbury could easily be mine. I had no idea why Mother thought Stuart would have opinions on the purchase, he had no interest in wireless sets at all.

*

The battery for my triode valve had been Mr Bonar's suggestion. At the conclusion of one of his "additional algebra" lessons the previous year, he had asked whether we would be interested in joining an Amateur Radio Club. He explained that such a club did not actually exist, but he had it in mind to teach a group of boys the morse code and see whether the school might eventually operate an amateur radio station. The club expired during its first meeting (it had at that point a membership of three) following Mr Bonar's account of the morse code practice necessary to reach even the modest target of five words per minute. Nonetheless, the group continued, and even gained members, in another, far more engaging, form. I had told Mr Bonar about my crystal set and he suggested that since we were not to become radio "hams", he could, at least, show us how to add a simple amplifier to a crystal set and tune in to their messages. We may not know what they meant, but we would hear morse code in action.

The list of war surplus things he asked us to find included "functioning triode valve" and the following week I arrived, proudly bearing my *Marconi* chassis, complete with its triode valve, loftily explaining that I knew the owner of the shop well and he had picked out this piece of army surplus gear specially for me. Mr Bonar took it off me, swivelling it round in his hands, mumbling, *Navy actually, but it will do very well. You'll need the HT battery. 120 volts.* This was the battery in the window of the Wednesbury shop, priced at twelve shillings and sixpence - way beyond what even pooled resources might have produced, now miraculously ours, thanks to Mother's five-pound notes.

*

Mr Bonar was one of two masters in the school charged to teach us mathematics. The contrast between these two could not have been more striking. Mr Carter had seemed relatively benevolent on my very first day at school, but this had been illusory. He conducted his classes in an atmosphere of supressed terror. His lessons comprised a kind of intellectual assault course, insoluble questions lobbed at random to petrified pupils - booby-trapped missiles, inevitably condemning the recipient to additional homework. This was the Mr Carter, you may recall, whose passion for quadratic equations had blighted my bonfire night some years before.

Mr Bonar, on the other hand, spent his harassed days battling boys rowdy to the point of riot. It was impossible to gain much from his lessons because they were rarely audible. Before the relief of my hospital sojourn, indiscipline in his A level class in calculus, had teetered so close to insurrection that neighbouring masters, fearful for his well-being, peered in from the corridor to discover their colleague at his lonely blackboard, chalk in hand, apparently drowning in a sea of riotous youth. Singing was not unknown. Strangely, no boy was ever asked to go and stand outside, none reprimanded, none set additional work; none, ever, invited to make that ominous journey beyond the green door. It was difficult to ignore one consequence of this appetite for riot - I made no progress in calculus and lamented more than ever the decision to commit my life to science.

Fortunately, there were too few of us in the re-styled Radio Club to misbehave. Armed with a slightly misshapen, but functioning, 120-volt battery we passed several contented lunch hours with Mr Bonar, squeezed into a tiny room, an annexe to the Physics Laboratory, bearing the impressive painted sign on its door *Preparation*, although we were never to discover what, if anything, was prepared there. Mr Bonar talked to us as to some benevolent unseen companion, walking back and forth between a chalked diagram on his portable blackboard and the pile of components laid out on the bench. Questions were answered in a casual companionable way as exchanges between interested equals and I began to look forward to these meetings. I learned a little physics, but learned a great deal more about this strange man, fashioned in the style of a Furnivall-the-Young, contentedly mumbling to himself in a haze of hot soldering flux. Above all, I solved the mystery of his otherwise inexplicable tolerance of manic levels of indiscipline. There was, in fact, no mystery to be solved - an endless procession of delinquents sent to The Pot would serve only to condemn the man who sent them. Unwilling to exert authority, he had trapped himself with no authority to exert. The Pot's retribution would have only confirmed his views on the vacuity of the subject taught and the wretched boys misguided enough to have chosen it. I had barely believed her when Joan described the intellectual caste system which ruled our school, a hierarchy of merit in which, somehow, Virgil would always get the final word. I believed her now.

*

The battered Marconi chassis being my contribution to the Radio Club, I was permitted to connect a small battery to illuminate the triode valve. It seemed improbable, but its gratifying yellow glow brought the web of soldered objects on the bench to life. Not, in fact, to present us with anything in morse code (it could not be tuned that high) but an episode of *Workers' Playtime*, clearly audible, serving just as well; someone singing *One Fine Day* from *Madame Butterfly* was greeted with enthusiastic applause. That song was often on the wireless. *Don't turn it off Bob,* Mother would say, *I want to listen.* And she would sit in rapt silence to its bitter end, her eyes filled with tears.

The assembled elements, complete with my functioning triode valve were donated to the Physics Laboratory as a final testimony to Mr Bonar's short-lived Radio Club. He would never have made a convincing tyrant and we could see he lacked whatever quirk of nature endowed Major Delauney with his effortless authority. But the ability to convert abstractions on a blackboard to physical reality defined him as a quite extraordinary teacher. With that in mind it fell to me to propose the *Silence Game* to the rebellious calculus class knowing they would agree, if only as a concession to Kenners, recently raised from his bed of pain.

Calculus had been relegated (possibly because of the association with Bedlam) to a remote classroom furnished with desks blackened with age, still bearing the gouged initials of long-departed pupils of another century. Most had retained their capacious Victorian china inkwells, easily big enough for miniature chemical experiments or even modest camp fires fashioned from matchsticks. There was nothing of the sort on the appointed day. Installed in my habitual back-row place, my signal brought the class to order as Mr Bonar arrived. He took his astonished place on the dais in a profound silence.

The lesson concerned the relationship between the sine and cosine of the angles of a right-angled triangle. Aware that we were entirely innocent of a long series of prior proofs and apparently puzzled to hear his own voice, he offered to set the lesson aside and refresh our collective memory. What followed was one of the most remarkable lessons any of us would ever hear. He drew a right-angled triangle on the board, asking us to consider the consequences of bringing one or another angle as close to zero as possible. Speaking in quiet conversational tones I recognised from the Radio Club, sketching possibilities as he spoke, he filled the board. True, the self-imposed silence was broken soon enough, but only to pose questions. Questions none of us had ever imagined asking, implying more than we realised we knew. Questions about the meaning of infinity; what it meant to divide by nothing; how nothing could exist; why some functions, but not others, strangely revealed themselves as slices cut across a cone. It ended finally, and we trouped out in the oddly exhilarated silence that sometimes followed one of the better Chapel sermons - a voluntary would have not been out of place. We felt curiously chastened.

No one agreeing to the *Silence Game* had imagined it might become permanent, but some strange social alchemy meant Mr Bonar's calculus classes were never restored to the mayhem of old. The following class was conducted again in an atmosphere of good-natured calm and we grew to like it. We had, in fact, discovered a congenial teacher with a surprising sense of humour, a willingness to talk to us on equal terms, and an eccentric affection for Wolverhampton Wanderers football team. By virtue of my occasional efforts at prefectorial *badinage*, I became a kind of class mascot, not unwilling to lighten the mood or pose the question no one dared to ask.

The school now boasted its own canteen, but a remnant of sandwich boys persisted, allowed to eat their lunch in the classroom. Calculus classes were held immediately after the lunch break and on one particular Thursday, Mother still being on her Malvern farm, I arrived with sandwiches constructed in a style Father dimly recalled from his Scouting days, to find a group of boys engaged in an impromptu competition. They had discovered a confiscated canteen table knife lying on the master's desk. Some of them had been to see *Treasure Island* that week and they were attempting to impale the knife into the wooden blocks of the floor, accompanying the efforts with parrot cries of *pieces-of-eight*. Knife-throwing seemed somewhat below the dignity of a prefect but I agreed to take my turn.

Intending simply to drop the knife to the floor, I clambered onto the seat of a desk to get the necessary height. It slipped neatly between two of the wooden blocks, tilted over in the slot, and snapped in two.

Mr Bonar found the broken pieces where they had been placed on his desk and asked for the culprit to identify himself. I recall standing to say, *it was I*, in a passable imitation of John Howard Davies in one of the more affecting scenes from *Tom Brown's Schooldays* and being told to wait behind. There ensued two of the most uncomfortable hours I have spent in my life. The cane was not yet outlawed at King Edward's and The Pot had actually wielded it last year for the sin of suspending a floral chamber pot from a particularly conspicuous window facing the High Street, although possibly the placard reading *Up The Pot* was judged equally culpable. He would certainly see wanton damage to school property - *stolen* school property – as quite culpable enough.

Mr Bonar had made no further reference to the broken knife and by the time the door had slammed behind the last departing mathematician, a deflated class mascot had already determined his fate could not be less than expulsion. Since I had temporarily lost the ability to stand, he had picked up the pieces of broken knife and perched himself on the desk in front of mine. It was only then that he smiled. A smile redolent of the wicker cane of St Mark's and a haze of pipe tobacco smoke, a million years ago. A familiar, peculiar, knowing, smile that brought such a tide of relief in its wake, I felt my eyes smarting. It was a curious exchange, neither looking at the other.

I'd say take the bits away, but they're not yours, are they, Kennedy?

Silence

And you'd end up in worse trouble.

Silence

I don't suppose you'll do it again.

Silence

So we'll leave it like that then.

Chapter 19

Ocker Hill Chapel had not, in fact, discovered a new organist while I had been in hospital; my first tentative visit for practice found the organ console I had already learned to think of as my own, dusty and untouched. Mr Gittens, who had been accompanying the congregation from the piano, greeted me with reports of a titanic theological dispute, still unresolved, adding mysteriously that, as the organist, I would soon enough be in the thick of it.

It had begun over a year ago when the Minister had reluctantly agreed that the Women's Institute annual Service of Dedication take place in the Methodist Chapel rather than at St Mark's, notwithstanding his suspicion that the officers of the Women's Institute did not share his enthusiastic support for the Labour Party. The current impasse concerned his denial of a request for the service to conclude in the customary fashion with the congregation singing Blake's *Jerusalem*. He brooked no argument on the matter: *Jerusalem* was not to be found in the Methodist Hymnal, for the obvious reason that it was not a hymn. Faced with the argument that other congregations had no such reservations, he broadened his objection. William Blake was not a Methodist, or even, strictly speaking, a Christian. Life for the poor of Ocker Hill was bad enough, it was cruel, perhaps even sinful, to hold out vague romantic hopes to the hopeless - that was exactly the kind of fanatical mystical thinking that John Wesley himself had always deplored. Utopia was all very well for those who could afford it, but we had more practical concerns. Our duty was to try to improve the drains in Toll End Road, not sit about hoping angels would dig them. No, he would not lend his office to the dissemination of Swedenborgian heresy and that was that.

Clearly, there were aspects of Methodism for which I was ill-prepared and I dreaded the Minister seeking my opinion. I knew a little about William Blake but in common with the bemused members of the Walsall Women's Institute, I had never heard of Swedenborg. To my relief, on the following Sunday, a smiling Minister declared that although any kind of ecclesiastic compromise had never been possible, he had found a way of accommodating our visitors. The heretical poem would play no role in the service, which would end with his own benediction. He handed me a bulky folder with *WI* stencilled on the cover, *but that still leaves the organist's voluntary*. If members of the Women's Institute want to stay and sing, he said, they were very welcome to do so. He seemed extraordinarily pleased with this somewhat Jesuitical solution, simply mumbling *a problem?* as he saw me anxiously leafing through the pages of sheet music in the folder. I shook my head, but he must have guessed I was lying. A single glance at the elaborate setting had been enough. The service was next week and it was extremely improbable I could learn to play it in time.

*

Sir Hubert Parry's setting of the poem *Jerusalem - for Organ and Unison Chorus*, although written in the depths of the Great War in 1916, is in the key of D major, a key Bach associated with triumph. Accordingly, it opens with an introductory flourish for organ solo, marked uncompromisingly *fff* in the music I had been given. Possibly not since its inauguration would the congregation of Ocker Hill chapel have heard their organ played *fortissimo*, for the simple reason that the instrument Messrs Norman and Beard had bequeathed them was capable, quite literally, of shaking the foundations of a building that had been erected, like everything else in Ocker Hill, over a honeycomb of slowly subsiding mine-workings. I bore my folder of music home thinking, not for the first time, of the *Pixie's Polka*.

There are more hours in the day when you are sixteen and I recall spending virtually all of them in the following week at the organ console. In a deserted chapel with no heating and only the light of the music stand, I found my way, inch by inch, into Parry's triumphal music, blithely unaware that the whole village had been in a position to gauge my progress, since every painful step was more than audible. To my dismay, I arrived for practice early on Saturday morning to discover the organ tuners already installed and likely to be there for the rest of the day. The foreman, who was busy stacking my music to one side, glanced at the sheets still propped up on the console and asked for a performance. He may have meant it as a joke, but I seized the opportunity for one final rehearsal. That is how it came about that a little group of men in dusty blue overalls were the first in many a year to hear in full voice the organ they were about to tune. I was sent back home with nods of approval – more for the instrument than the organist – and a solemn promise from the foreman *to do something about that trumpet for you.*

That Sunday I came of age as an organist, although all I remember of the service were the words of the Minister's benediction, my sacred signal. Barely aware that I was responsible for sounds that had suddenly brought the place alive, I found myself singing in some other world, brighter than Ocker Hill ever was. Singing in concert with numberless other voices, bellowing words I did not know I knew, words that had somehow seeped into my consciousness in all those long hours of practice. I have no idea how long it took – strictly speaking, I was not sure I was even present – but for whatever time it was, I knew with a strange certainty that our Minister, for all he meant well, was simply wrong. Blake's haunting invocation to a better place was not some romantic dream at all. Indeed, if Jerusalem could not be built in Ocker Hill, it could not be built anywhere. Methodists make much of the vision which changed the life of Saint Paul. I had a vision of my own, albeit on a smaller scale, that afternoon. More than a little drunk on music and taxed beyond my strength by the heavy coupling of the organ, I realise now I had suffered a seizure of some kind. But what I had briefly seen in that performance has never left me all my life - that mountains are worth climbing, even if few or none can live there. They are worth climbing for the view.

The service over, I closed the organ desk and sat for a while, weak with exhaustion. I could see the Minister in the vestry from where I sat, but conscious he would resent that I had secured some kind of victory, I decided it would be awkward to go out that way. The congregation had left and I made my way down the aisle thinking of Saint Paul. It was not, in fact, completely deserted; two people were sitting together near the back, apparently waiting. As I drew closer, one of them stood up and eased the folder of music from my hands with a motherly smile: *Mildred here says you were practising for days. Well, you had your reward - it was splendid.*

I walked out of the Chapel side by side with Mildred. Almost unconsciously we took up the old Sunday walk, threading our familiar devious route down Gospel Oak Road to avoid watching eyes. She said she had written to me at the hospital but the letter had been sent back, although she did not say what she had written. Apparently, the vicar of St Mark's had put my name in the Parish Magazine saying that I was in hospital and our Minister had asked for me to be remembered at the morning service when there was nobody to play the organ. When I said I never knew any of this, she took my hand and held on even as I pulled away a little. I felt awkward hand-in-hand with a girl at my side, almost as if we were walking out, justifying it to myself as an invitation to expand on my theological dispute with the Minister.

She walked at my side, pausing now and then to snatch at flowering weeds along the path with her free hand, listening to my thoughts on William Blake. The divine, I solemnly declared, had nothing to do with churches, organs, or the Women's Institute for that matter, it was a part of human nature, hastily adding *if we want it to be*, because I could see the philosophical pit I was digging for myself. She said Mr Ableson had already explained that the question of whether God was within or without was insoluble, *and could we talk about something else?* She was taking Scripture at A level and I assumed this condescending critic was one of her teachers, but she would say no more. I had rather been hoping she would talk about *Jerusalem*.

*

I caught the same bus as Ian the day Mother came back from Malvern. She was in the kitchen with Stuart and a woman I had never seen before. They had been talking, but stopped when we arrived. Mother looked pleased to see us but Stuart seemed irritated when we slumped into our respective chairs and began looking for the day's delivery of *The Eagle* comic. The three of them stood in a little group as if waiting for us to go away so that they could go on with what they were talking about. Mother told us to shake hands with Grace and said she had got to know her at the hospital and that Grace was poorly and needed a rest. She asked us whether we had any homework to do, which was strange because she knew we always had homework to do. Stuart told Ian to take his *Eagle* into the front room and gave me a prod until I followed him. I remember I got my homework out but sat doing nothing at all, wondering what they were talking about and why Mother had said *hospital*. She couldn't have meant my hospital because nobody came there.

We never really discovered who Grace was. Stuart, adopting his doctor's voice, said we must ask Father, but for reasons we could hardly have articulated, neither of us ever did. We had both seen Father, cigarette in hand, anxiously pacing the garden path where, years before, he had broken our cricket bat and concluded he was better where he was. For several days this mysterious woman would appear to sit in awkward silence with Mother, the two of them waiting until we went away and they could resume their urgent conversation.

The visits ended as abruptly as they had begun. After about a fortnight Mother told us Grace would never come again because she had died. It would be a while before I would encounter death on my own account and, as with Uncle Leslie, hearing of it at second hand in this way, I was lost to know what I should say, still less what I should feel. I pieced a little of the story together over the following week. Stuart let drop that Malvern had not suited Mother after Auntie Bessie had left her there and her seizures had started again. She had spent a day in the hospital at Wolverhampton for tests and had met Grace there. He would not say what the tests were for, although I think he knew I guessed. All I am sure of is that Mother's tears that day were tears of anger: Grace, I was to know, had not deserved what had befallen her and since I spent my time praying, I could tell that to God - not that he'd care.

*

Each Sunday now I would find Mildred waiting in her accustomed pew after the morning voluntary and I began to look forward to our literary discussions along the canal bank. I recall one such walk when she delivered a parcel to her Auntie Ivy because, living at the foot of Leabrook Road, avoiding number 160 involved a long and circuitous approach. They stood on the doorstep talking, a little apart from me, occasional glances in my direction leaving me with an uneasy sense I was being appraised.

Inevitably, I was late back for dinner. Mother went to fetch something she'd left for me in the kitchen and stood over me at the dining table while I ate, breaking a rather ominous silence to ask why I was still mooning after that girl in Toll End Road. *And there's no point denying it, because Ian had seen me.* The claim that Mildred was doing English at school and that we talked about poets like William Blake secured little relief from the inquisition. Ignoring my brazen declaration of the offending name, Mother demanded what was I thinking of, letting myself play second fiddle to a girl like that? And what was she to do when this girl's mother started crowing about it to the whole village? And the way her mother went on, that was bound to happen, *and your father won't have it.* I blurted out that all my troubles lay at Father's door, it was his fault I was taking subjects I didn't like. It was him who wanted me to be an apprentice. Why could I not do English like all my friends at school? Since even Mother knew this could not possibly be true, I realised I had said too much. Who, exactly, could these *friends* be? Or did I mean *friend*? Stuart said everybody knew about a girl in Stourbridge, and she was doing English. Who was this girl? Only the other day, Stuart had been joking with Father, she said: *One to wash and one to wear, your father had said. No, that would never do, would it?* Something in her voice as she said these last words made me crane round in my seat. A thin vindictive smile faded from her lips as she saw my desperate face, filled with thoughts of Joan: *Oh, Alan, is it like that? I'll write and ask. I'm sure they'll let you do what you want.*

*

It would very soon be Christmas. Each of my A level science courses had mutated in ways I found both more demanding and less interesting, hopes of dropping one of them in favour of English

154

literature withering fast. Soon it would be too late. It was the school Christmas Concert that year which proved my unlikely saviour, setting in train events which altered the course of my life.

The school's Cadet Force was organised by a certain Captain Maddox, an extremely diminutive man possessed of a florid face and a clipped military moustache. Albeit a conscientious teacher of English literature in the school, his willingness to appear every Thursday at Assembly immaculately kitted out as a kind of miniature soldier had earned him the strong disapproval of Major Delauney. The closest we had to a real soldier among us made no secret of his opposition to the very existence of a military wing in the school. So far as we could judge, the two men never exchanged words. As with Stuart, Father refused to sign the necessary papers for me to join the Cadet Force (an injunction Ian somehow evaded), but the cadets were already in steep decline at that time and I openly aligned myself with Major Delauney's scornful dismissal of *Maddox's toy soldiers*. Fearing I had taken sides a little too obviously, I was alarmed one day to be told to report to Captain Maddox without delay.

I found him in a quiet room I had long hoped to enter. Furnished with no more than a polished table with chairs along both sides, it was where A level students of English literature spent their golden hours. To my relief, Captain Maddox was not seeking retribution. On the contrary, he said he had heard good reports of my contribution to the Debating Society and would I have the time to prepare a monologue from Shakespeare's play *Richard II* and present it at the Christmas Concert? I would have to know it by heart, but it was only about forty lines and he was willing to coach me. He saw me greedily eyeing the book open at his side and took that as agreement enough, hastily adding that I would also need to find another boy who could call King Richard to meet Bolingbroke at the end of my monologue (that little "my" brought an instant glow of pleasure). Did I know of anyone, because we would need to rehearse together? As yet, unaware of his elevation to the Earldom of Northumberland, Bashforth was recruited on the spot.

I soon learned the speech, *What must the King do now?* and came to enjoy my sessions with Captain Maddox as he patiently explained some of the nuances of Richard II. Almost, it seemed, if only for an hour or two, I became a student of literature and relished it. My costume, hired for the occasion, was a professional affair, including an enveloping garment in lurid gold, a little like an over-size dressing gown; red and gold slippers of a vaguely Turkish design; a crown; a sceptre; and a small wooden plaque that I was instructed to look at in a wistful way when I offered to exchange my subjects for a pair of carvèd saints. Since there was no costume for Bashforth, we decided he would address King Richard from the front of the Hall, a Modernist touch that allowed me to make my exit, descending from the stage *like glist'ring Phaëton* and out through The Pot's habitual morning door - a decision destined to cost me dear.

*

My allotted place in the programme gave me the right to attend rehearsals in the few days before Christmas and witness what was to become the *succès de scandale* of the year. A few of the more muscular members of the rugby first fifteen had hit on the notion of dressing up as High School girls and performing *I Love to Go A-wandering*. This curiously Hitlerian hiking song had been made popular at the time by a recording (in German) by the Oberkirchen Children's Choir. Equivalent English choirs had taken up the challenge and it was impossible at that time to avoid the quasi-yodelling refrain: *Val-de-ri, Val-de-ra, Val-de ha ha ha ha ha ha*. The rugby players, ten in all, decided to copy a television cabaret style of presentation in which a line of dancers, each clutching her neighbour's waist, progress sideways by means of high kicking steps. The audition earned smiles even from the master in charge, who, given the intention to dress as schoolgirls, set in train an elaborate approval process involving The Pot himself. Propriety was eventually satisfied by placing two teachers from the Dame School in charge of "dressing." I already knew from conversations with Joan that the event was eagerly anticipated and more articles of clothing had been offered as props than could be used. The final costume for each burly youth comprised a wig topped by the winter version of the High School hat, unkindly known as a *flowerpot*; a High School blazer; white blouse; short summer skirt; voluminous hockey knickers in blue serge; and King Edward's School regulation rugby boots together with knitted socks in the school colours, where possible. A suitably rounded physique was achieved by means of *brassieres,* modestly padded with cotton wool by Miss Drury, although some boys improved on the effect.

The group had already begun rehearsals, when Brown - revealing an unsuspected talent for the theatrical - suggested that Kennedy participate. Since I weighed about a quarter of any of the others in the group and, even with padding, would be much less than half their width, he thought I could add a comic touch. He fashioned a kind of yellow wig from straw and pinned it under my flowerpot, producing the overall effect of an emaciated scarecrow. A painted mountain backdrop, *papier maché* boulders and an artful waterfall of silver beads completed the set. Brown took in hand the choreography, based very roughly on the work of Busby Berkeley in which, as denouement, I emerged from a rugby scrum of blue serge like Venus from her shell.

It was only during the first of several rather chaotic dress rehearsals that I recalled something Captain Maddox had mentioned at our final Shakespearian meeting. The monologue, he explained, would have to be performed in front of the curtain while the set and performers for the next act were readied on the stage; he could not see it presenting a problem. He was wrong, of course, because the next act in question was the girls' choir and it was difficult to see how I could appear in both. I had, however, underestimated the combined ingenuity of Bashforth and Brown. After due reflection, they arrived at a solution. As agreed, King Richard II would descend into the Hall and make his exit stage right. Once through the door, he would run along the colonnade outside, through the gate to Mr Carpenter's garden, along a few yards of the High Street, and up the stone staircase in time to join the chorus, stage left. I wouldn't have time to change my shoes, but Turkish slippers would do perfectly well.

I had managed my monologue rather better in rehearsals with Captain Maddox, but it went off well enough, with a ripple of applause as, summoned by Bashforth from the front row of the audience, King Richard made his stately way down the stairs and out through The Pot's door. Thereafter, my memory is hazy, but I reflected later that night on what the bus queue might have made of a slight, but kingly, figure haring along the High Street, complete with crown, sceptre and modestly padded *brassière*. I shall never know. That I had played my part in the Oberkirchen Choir was reward enough.

On the following Monday, our little troupe was personally congratulated by The Pot, who asked me to stay behind for a moment. He said I no doubt knew my mother had written about the possibility of my doing English. Careful examination of the timetable suggested that, of the three science subjects I was studying, it would be possible for me to discontinue chemistry. He had spoken to Captain Maddox, who would allow me to join the class he was preparing for the A level examinations in English literature. He did not think the choice very sensible, and I would still miss some lessons, but given what my mother had said, he would not stand in my way. I never knew what she had written.

Chapter 20

I had worried that a late-comer to Literature would be seen as an interloper, but enough boys had been at the school concert to ensure me a reasonable welcome. I discovered all I needed to know about Captain Maddox's eccentric approach to teaching at that first meeting. Although defacing books was close to a hanging offence in the school, he had given each member of his class permission to transcribe footnotes into their copies of *The Winter's Tale*, artfully ensuring that an otherwise tedious activity was charged with a permanent aura of transgression. Ordered to follow each reference to its bitter end, into another play if need be, it was not long before the margins of my own book were as dense with illegal ink as all the others.

The class was ruthlessly Socratic, Captain Maddox scrawling a question on the board and pursuing us in turn until we arrived at an answer he considered satisfactory. I arrived at my first class, a little late, to find: *If Leontes is Othello in this play, who is Iago?* It took most of the morning to decide it was Leontes himself, but by then I had discovered that the solution counted for very little – it was the discussion that mattered. Utterly seduced, I left that first meeting light-headed with the pleasures of juvenile scholarship and happier than I had been for months.

*

I discovered the Chess Club had played – and won - two away games while I was in hospital. Unwilling to humble myself and petition to rejoin, I let my membership lapse. The "thirteen-plus" boy who had taken my place was also giving up. He said he now played the accordion for his father's Morris dance group and was far too busy for chess. Mike lived somewhat in the Durrell family style in a vast farmhouse in the wilds of Warwickshire. Like most of the Steiner boys who joined the school mid-stream, he was a talented musician; his performance in the school concert had almost overshadowed the children from Oberkirchen: a bravura recital involving tenor, alto and bass recorders, concluding with something by Scarlatti for the sopranino instrument.

I found his attachment to folklore and Morris dancing congenial. The dawn of the vaunted New Elizabethan Age had proved a disappointment to Ocker Hill, and the dances and nursery rhymes of an earlier and merrier England offered a measure of solace in our reconstructed desolation. For someone who now spent days which might have been devoted to chemistry, fruitlessly trying to unravel Shakespeare's sonnets, it was but a small step to join the Folklore Society (albeit as a Junior Member, which was cheaper) and find consolation in the works of Cecil Sharp and Peter Opie, much as *Rupert the Bear of Nutwood* had comforted my earliest war-time years.

It was only when I conveyed the information to Mother, that I realised Mike would be the first King Edward's boy I had invited to Ocker Hill. Neither Brown nor Bashforth had visited Leabrook Road, largely because the contrast between the carpeted splendour of their homes and the shabby linoleum of my own left me too ashamed. This visitor, I was certain, would find such considerations beneath his concern - I had not reflected on exactly *how* I knew this remarkable fact, but it had much to do with Morris dancing. Mother provided egg and watercress sandwiches and Father joined us for what proved a pleasant meal, Mike distributing his golden words between the two, but attending most to Mother. Although she was plainly disappointed that my first visitor had not been a particular girl, she thawed under the spell of his effortless aristocratic charm. Earnestly nodding, he sat in patient attentive silence for what seemed like hours, hearing out the garrulous parade of all the little triumphs of my apparently endless life.

We walked together to the Chapel and Mike sat in the balcony while I played the organ for him. I learned a great deal that afternoon, swapping places to discover the sound of the instrument as the congregation heard it. By the time we set off home we had resolved to seek out fellow musicians at school and form a band of some kind, possibly an accordion band: we might even earn money playing for "square dances" in the region – the craze of the moment.

When we got back, I looked for Ian's battered descant recorder and Mike gave a recital, followed by an impromptu demonstration of Morris dancing, pounding up and down the living room in a cloud of dust, flicking a pair of handkerchiefs dangerously close to our single suspended electric light bulb. When he finished, Mother clapped, for want of anything else to do and Mike, breathing heavily, bowed and asked whether I would like to join the group. Father had been watching in astonished silence and his *NO!* was possibly louder and more emphatic than he intended, but he made no effort to ease the ensuing awkward silence. Finally, Mother mumbled she would put the kettle on for tea. But it was too late: Mike said he had to be getting home.

With the visitor gone, Father's pent-up rage poured out: I had rarely seen him so angry. If I wanted to dance, why didn't I go with Stuart to the dance at the College in Dudley? What's more, find somebody to take, not this stuck-up clown. *A proper pansy he looked, jumping about like that.* And what was all this my mother was saying about changing courses? And no doubt ending up doing something no use at all; something I could do at any school. I was making a fool of myself, parading about with a boy like that. He slammed out of the room without letting me speak. It was the most he had said to me in years – we had settled of late on something slightly less than a truce, avoiding all but customary words, and those as rarely as possible. At first, it seemed his anger reflected some primordial panic, born of my girlish past; fear I had fallen prey to an improbably youthful Montague. But as I sat on, hearing the kitchen cupboards bang I realised his antipathy to Mike had little to do with dancing and even less with sex. He had watched the two of them talking, seen the pretence in Mike's attention to Mother's pointless meandering words, and despised him for it. I realised how deeply he had resented Mike's innocent wink in my direction as she had turned to look for something about levitation in her *Prediction* magazine. Father had - perhaps for the first time - seen her through someone else's eyes; seen her as we boys had come to know her now every day; seen the truth of Mother's diminished state; and hated Mike for revealing it.

161

*

Sunday walks with Mildred after chapel now occasionally included a mid-day meal, invariably roast chicken, a weekly offering from her uncle's surprising turkey farm in the suburbs of Wolverhampton, eaten in a style I recognised from the regrettable episode of the mended cup, plates precariously perched on our laps. Although her parents knew I was the chapel organist, they had no idea how I spent my days and had reluctantly accepted me as some suitably distant friend of their daughter. I think had they sniffed romance in the matter I would have been sent packing. Probably they imagined she had taken pity on someone doomed to join the ranks of itinerant Methodist preacher-organists who could still eke out a living, even then. It had already been decided Mildred would become the village teacher, usurping Mother's place and securing recompense for her theatrical pretentions.

I owed my accordion to Mildred. I had told her some time ago of the ambition to form a band and she said her mother had seen an accordion for sale in the *small ads* section of the Saturday edition of *The Express and Star*. A few days later we travelled together by bus to a bungalow in the remote hinterland of Cradley Heath, where, for the sum of ten pounds, ten shillings, I took possession of a Hohner instrument in the piano style with 60 bass keys, three ranks of reeds, and case. Although it never lost the scent of its deceased owner's cigarettes, it was in perfect condition; I did not regret parting with Mother's remaining five-pound notes.

It is one thing to own a piano accordion and certainly quite another to play it, and my earliest efforts were dispiriting. Incredibly heavy, it could only be played standing up, and its keyboard, stretching vertically down to somewhere approaching my knees, was necessarily invisible. The keys were narrow and locating which to play so demanding, I would often forget to provide the necessary air pressure and produce no sound at all apart from a vacant succession of clicks. The bass buttons, played with the left hand, were designed to produce chords (major, minor and diminished seventh) and although I was never at all proficient, I mastered them sufficiently to produce simple accompaniments to folk dance tunes. Within a few

162

weeks, Mike had assembled the nucleus of his band: lead accordion; double bass; clarinet; guitar; and piano. By the time of its first public performance, by virtue of heroic hours of practice in the Leabrook Road kitchen, the second accordionist was added, capable of "doubling" the melody and adding a tentative, if not wholly accurate, bass accompaniment.

The congregation of St Mark's church, Ocker Hill, restricted their social gatherings to whist drives and amateur dramatics, so I did not encounter organised dancing until I joined the heathen Methodists. Even then, it was only to discover forms of dance long since lost to antiquity elsewhere. Mine was surely the last generation to witness country dances and *quadrilles* artlessly performed in ways Thomas Hardy would have found familiar. The *Valeta Waltz*, danced at arm's length, was the only concession to modernity accepted by the chapel elders of Ocker Hill.

Mike had amassed a sufficient repertoire of tunes suited to these ancient dances - *Sir Roger de Coverley, The Shepherd's Hey, The Cuckoo's Nest,* and so forth – that he allowed me to declare the school band available, at no cost, to perform at the next social dance, replacing the portable gramophone. If not an unqualified triumph, the magical lure of live music was enough to earn us a second invitation, although by then we were in demand, performing most weekends in schools, youth clubs, and church halls, venturing on occasion as far afield as West Bromwich and sometimes earning as much as a pound note each. Bashforth played the clarinet in the band and, since they were inseparable, Brown came with him as psychological support. With nothing else to do, he joined the dancing, Mildred making up the numbers as his partner. They danced well together. If I was courting Mildred at that time – I was never very sure about that – we rarely met without my bringing with me a second, and equally undecided, suitor.

*

I confidently expected Joan to be pleased by my sudden accession to the world of English letters and prepared for the Saturday of the next play reading by composing six sonnets. Written over the previous weeks, in a style owing much to Walter de la Mare, but with Shakespearian borrowings, I was inordinately proud of these poems, suffused as they were with latent passion. One, at least, came close to a daring declaration and despite Brown's professional opinion - the single word *tosh* - I carefully stapled them together with a cardboard cover. Joan glanced briefly at the first and handed the little package back with, *I knew you'd start getting airs.* She flatly refused to discuss Shakespeare with me, saying there were more pressing matters to talk about. Brown had petitioned her again to join the play-readers and the two of them had been talking about our band. She had known Mike's family for years - how did I come to know him and she not to know? It was a complicated question which I realised had something else hidden inside, but she did not even wait for an answer. When was she going to hear the band? Although, on second thoughts, she wasn't sure she had the time. That was our last Kardomah meeting. I remember her handing me her little yellow booklet, saying she was tired of play reading, and would I ask Frenchie to read her part because she wasn't going. Half out of her chair, she leaned across to say *I always knew you'd be a waste of time,* brushing my cheek with her lips. I suppose it was a kiss of a kind.

*

That was the summer Mother had her operation. Mike's visit had seemed a kind of watershed in her battle with *melancholia*. As the days after his visit passed, she spoke less and less, sitting silently at the dining table, eating whatever Father put before her. The meal over, she would return to her habitual chair by the fire to stare into space. For a while she asked about Mike, but he never visited the house again, and soon she barely spoke at all. The wireless irritated her, even things we had listened to for years, her mumbled *turn it off, Bob* reducing the house to silence. A doctor came, someone I had never seen before. Urgent whispered consultations with Father and Stuart resumed in the front room. By then, Mother had taken to her bed and the doctor would dash upstairs to see her almost as an afterthought. Her *melancholia*, he said, was very much worse.

Perhaps the operation itself was as brief as Stuart had said - I never discovered – but Mother was away for several days, returning with Father late one afternoon. He shepherded her in, his hands not quite touching her back, as if at any moment she might fall. She had brought with her into the room an antiseptic smell and stood looking at us one by one, finally settling weary darkened eyes on me. My heart thumping with a kind of terror, I saw her turn to the husband she seemed barely to know, smiling a smile not quite her own: *that's Alan, isn't it?*

All this was seventy years ago. I never knew where the operation was carried out; Wolverhampton, I assume. Long discontinued, the name, *trans-orbital leucotomy*, buried a barbaric practice under imposing words. A blade inserted in the upper part of the orbit of the eye and through a barrier of bone cuts the cortex, severing links to deeper structures in the brain. All this effected by the surgeon - for that was how he termed himself - wielding an instrument like a tiny double-facing axe - the *icepick*, as they termed it, in the theatre banter of that time. Anaesthetic was not judged necessary since the procedure was preceded by an electro-convulsive stimulus and the patient would remember nothing. The surgeon knew, albeit approximately, where his blade would cut, but as to knowing *which* cells were then destroyed, that was, admittedly, a challenge: there are around sixteen billion nerve cells in the cortex.

That was the day my mother went away. Whoever returned with Father that afternoon, looked much as Mother had always looked, and in the weeks that followed, whoever it was, recovered enough to ape her habitual turns of speech. But of the two, I alone now possessed the life we once had shared: her part in it had altogether gone. That is a lesson learned a thousand times, yet never learned – that memories re-created, however lovingly, are never memories *restored*, nor can they be. For all your earnest hopes, the person you believe you know is fated to reveal she is no more than some cruel likeness. Not the Dutchess Anastasia, after all.

And what of the men who did this dreadful thing? No better than the savage tribesmen of another age, innocent of cinema, frantically spearing images on the screen. *Melancholia* for Freud was mourning in another guise; only madmen, he said, would look to surgery to heal the pain of grief. Did these madmen truly believe that in severing tissue they could unstitch the fabric of my mother's mind, pulling at just the melancholic threads? Had they thought to ask, they might have learned more exactly why she was transfixed by Madama Butterfly's farewell to hope - she must have wept a thousand times hearing that. Had they any idea how small a part *hope* had ever played in her war-damned life? I had heard *One Fine Day* improbably emerge from Mr Bonar's tiny crystal set. Could these surgeons possibly believe they would discover hope in a triode valve?

Chapter 21

It must have been about a month after Mother's operation. She knew us all by then, although she mixed our names up, always saying it didn't matter. She had begun to walk a little outside with Stuart, even as far as the newspaper shop, and she had not done that for a long time. Mrs Furnivall stopped to say how pleased she was to see her out and about, but Mother, speaking far too loud, had said she didn't know who this woman was and asked Stuart to take her home. The doctor said her *melancholia* had gone, although Father seemed bewildered that so many other things had gone as well that it hardly seemed a cure. They should have explained, he said, that her seizures would never go away and she would always need her medicine: it was a disappointment. But she had been lucky, the doctor said, really lucky; often, the operation made the seizures worse.

Perhaps because we had been so much a pair, I failed to come to terms with this new person in our house, settling for a life in which pretence loomed large. Father, traumatised more than he knew, warily pondered what the doctor's word *lucky* yet might bring, while Ian, still too young to care, adopted a kind of bantering exchange with our new Mother that she seemed to like. It was Stuart who mastered our changed way of being, closer now than he had ever been before, the two endlessly locked in mumbled kitchen conversation. As Father, all those long years ago, had strangely foreseen, our own doctor had come to govern the house.

I recall a conversation about Mother with Stuart at that time. I had dared to say that she knew so little of our life before – nothing really - that I barely knew who she was. Before her operation, at least she knew when she had forgotten something - *it will come to me*, she would say, and often it did. It was not like that now: she did not mourn the things that had gone, and seemed not to care. One question above all vexed me - if she did not know the things she had lost, why would she want them back? How, then, could she ever return? Stuart, already possessed of daunting medical gravitas, said I was being perverse. It was easy for me to talk - what mattered was that her *melancholia* had gone. Did I want her misery to return? As for forgetting things, I knew perfectly well she had been like that for years, *so what really had changed?* I have been haunted by that question for much of my life.

*

Our first television set arrived at about the time of Mother's operation. I had seen very little television before then: the Coronation ceremony, on a set with a patent magnifier strapped to its tiny screen; and a few illicit encounters in Leabrook Road during the occasional absences of Mr and Mrs Walker, when their boys felt free to entertain in style. Stationed where a fire-side chair once had stood, it was impossible to see the Kennedy family's television set unless the curtains were drawn, effectively converting the room into a kind of claustrophobic theatre. I preferred to take my entertainment outdoors and fashioned a portable wireless in a wooden box, shaped like a small coffin. It was just about possible to lug this device and its attendant batteries into the neighbouring fields and receive the Light Programme transmission from Droitwich, *Paul Temple* a particular favourite.

Television captivated Mother much as a professional hypnotist might and for several years, two programmes in particular mesmerised her: test match cricket, watched for long hours in curtained gloom, although it was hard to believe she understood the rules; and *Come Dancing*, a ballroom dancing competition in which about thirty couples, in full evening dress, were whittled down over the course of a long evening, until a winner was declared. Father's secret younger sister, Auntie Winifred, was the partner of a professional ballroom dancer and the pair occasionally appeared on this programme, circling among the others like clockwork automata, Father tracking their progress with a finger on the screen. He said they were going to set up a dancing school and, *if I wanted to learn to dance properly, why didn't I ask my Auntie Winifred?*

In other times this innocent remark would have been a declaration of war. Although we had never seen her, we all knew that

Auntie Winifred lived in Grandfather Kennedy's pub, *The Waggon and Horses* in Great Bridge. Mother's ferocious disapproval of public houses in general, and that one in particular, had only increased on learning that Grandmother had taken up the licence when he died. So far as I recall, we were only allowed to visit once a year, as a christian concession and because the Prime Minister had wisely closed the pubs on Christmas Day. Even then, we had to walk the three miles to Great Bridge because there were no buses. There could have been no greater mark of the end of Mother's sway than this shameless reference to an aunt I had never met; what's more, one not greatly older than myself. Mother showed no sign she cared.

Nonetheless, the proposition lived with me: I had watched Mildred dancing with Brown and begun to appreciate drawbacks to the second accordionist's role. From my position on the stage, it had been impossible to ignore the degree of intimacy Brown somehow imported into otherwise innocent communal dances. Not that Mildred appeared to mind; there were even occasions when his chosen girlfriend of the night went home early. The prospect of Brown retreating in the face of my newly-acquired professional skill, was difficult to resist.

In fact, the professional concerned was not to be my aunt, as I had imagined, but her partner, Melvyn. On several successive Saturday afternoons, having helped shift the tables in the Saloon bar of *The Waggon and Horses* to make room, I learned the quickstep, including a rather complicated *fishtail* flourish. We danced to records of Victor Silvester's strict tempo band, me clasped to Melvyn's bosom in a tight embrace. Auntie Winifred occasionally poked her head round the door to watch, but I had to wait until my final day before it was deemed I had made sufficient progress to dance with her - albeit with stern warnings of what would befall me if I damaged her feet. I danced with her for a whole record, feather-light in my arms, aware through the touch of her body of her endless hours of rehearsal in every polished step. I walked home on air, thinking of Gene Kelly and hardly minding the rain.

*

I was, alas, fated never to demonstrate my quickstep skills, with or without its fishtail. My troubles began, innocently enough, with Sports Day, marking the end of my first year in the sixth form. Although I lived further away than almost every boy in the school, you may recall a rather bemused Mr Carter had assigned me on arrival to the School House, home of the muscular stars of rugby and cricket. Since I had no taste for either activity, and "athletics" provided legitimate – if highly suspect - grounds for avoiding both, I had contrived to become the principal representative for my house in middle-distance running. Hours at the organ had possibly endowed my legs with the strength to move a scandalously under-weight body at speed; whatever the reason, I could, with a minimum of training, comfortably win races at 220 and 440 yards, against plump opposition.

Having already won two races that year, bravado induced me to put my name forward as a late entrant for the 880-yard event. It proved to be a race too many, with catastrophic consequences. At the half-way point, I had sped so far ahead of the field that a glance over my shoulder revealed only a distant chasing group, still slipping back; it seemed I had only to saunter my way to the tape. I had misjudged the foresight necessary to saunter in a two-lap race, and as first one, then another, then all of them, loped past my exhausted form, I could do no more than watch. I hobbled in at something less than a painful walking pace, close to collapse, my only comfort a complete absence of spectators.

Although I felt unwell, the prospect of dazzling Brown with my quickstep, brought me later that day to the end-of-year dance at the Technical College in Dudley. Half my bus ride home, I arrived early and sat outside, feeling sick, my legs acutely aware of that final humiliating race. Eventually, a bus arrived from the other direction, bearing Mildred with Brown and his official girl *du jour*. I limped after them into the dancehall, to be confronted by a stunning wave of heat. Just visible, beyond a heaving mass of strangely gyrating humanity, a distant youthful band was playing *Rock around the Clock* as loudly as their instruments allowed, or possibly even louder. I stood in the doorway, aware that a new pain in my back had coupled itself to a paralysing headache: I would certainly be wise to go home. As I turned to leave, Brown had already grasped both women and hauled them into the throng for the fourth invocation to *rock*, leaving me to stagger out into the broad daylight of Dudley's Castle Hill. When last sighted, the three were energetically engaged in a communal dance I did not recognise, although it was clearly not the quickstep.

In an uncanny repetition of my experience of the year before, I reached 160, Leabrook Road barely able to put myself to bed and awoke from what must have been a prolonged feverish seizure, clutching my collected sonnets, although I have no idea how they came to be in my hand. Mother was pressing a familiar white enamel basin under my chin and I was promptly sick, only some of the blood-stained product reaching the basin. Father arrived to discover a scene not unlike David's portrayal of the death of Marat, as I strove, against all odds, to save my precious blood-stained verse.

It was not, this time, the *Fever Van* that bore me away to hospital, but a more substantial vehicle, summoned in haste by Dr Hildebrand. I remember seeing bright sunlight against windows that had been painted over in grey and wondering what had become of the night, Father kneeling among a tangled collection of metal contraptions on the floor alongside where I lay. I saw him crane round to ask the men what they thought was the matter, something in their refusal to reply frightening me. Mother had not come with him. I felt dreadfully ill.

*

Although they had every reason to suspect that I had indeed fallen victim to the plague of polio then stalking the Midlands, the ambulance men's mute pessimism proved unwarranted: I was not, as they had surely concluded, yet one more boy that year to be confined to his iron lung. In fact, an austere consultant, dressed as for a garden party, complete with tiny rosebud in his lapel, surveyed my naked frame shortly after my arrival, and declared he'd only seen this before in rowers. *Did I row?* He asked, barely pausing to add, *no, I can see you don't.* It appeared that this, my seventeenth summer, was to be stolen by *rhabdomyolysis*. I would have preferred a complaint that I could spell, or at least properly pronounce, but I listened as best I could to his laconic account of what had befallen me, noting that he had yet to say whether there was any prospect of cure. He said he could hear a murmur in my heart, but that was not what had laid me low - extreme exertion had released components of damaged muscle into my bloodstream, with dire consequences, one of which was acute renal failure. Still uncertain of my prognosis, several days passed before he added *Pyelonephritis* to the burgeoning clipboard suspended at my feet. I had been *harbouring* a low-level kidney infection for some time, he said, the word implying a degree of complicity in my own downfall. But all was not lost: treatment with tetracycline antibiotics would, with patience, eventually restore me to life.

Patience meant my second sojourn in Moxley Isolation Hospital was long enough to allow me to discover a single, somewhat sinister, exception to its procrustean visitation rules. Reluctantly accepting the notion of *Benefit of Clergy*, vicars of the Anglican persuasion were permitted to visit those of their parishioners whose stay was destined to be long, or possibly not long enough. I had been there for three weeks or so when Vicar Bell was ushered into my cell one afternoon by a nurse apparently under orders to stand guard at the open door. Without his octagonal hat, although dressed in austere black, he made no mention of this particular parishioner's defection to the Methodist cause, staring meaningfully at the guard until she delicately backed away, leaving us alone. He proceeded to pull out books from various pockets, piling them onto my bedside table. I remember little else about the visitation and he never returned, but when he left, the nurse examined my little library before briskly tidying the books away in a way that suggested it was not her first encounter with ecclesiastical smuggling. I kept them, appropriately enough, under the bible in my little cupboard and took them with me when I left, but they were hardly concealed and no one ever asked where they came from.

I was, at first, too poorly to read, my days plagued with fear that the doctors would add epileptic propensities to my collection of ailments and phenobarbital to the impressive list of drugs I was compelled to take. But the disease, or its treatment, effected a temporary end to seizures, and as a tide of anxiety ebbed, I began to take an interest in the vicar's clandestine texts. Three treasures:

my physics textbook, last seen on the bureau in Leabrook Road; a battered copy of *King Lear* with a "cancelled" library stamp; and a stubby book in a blue cover, entitled *The Oxford Book of Modern Verse*. The *Lear* was boldly annotated in Captain Madox's handwriting with the single word "footnotes", and from the smudged signature inside the anthology I deduced it had been his own copy, although he provided no instruction as to what I was to do with it. These three books comprised the total of my decidedly eccentric A level revision until the day of my discharge. And even that was not, as I had imagined, to return to Leabrook Road, but to begin a protracted period of convalescence.

*

I was not to convalesce alone. Mother came with me as a supplementary patient, the two of us installed for several weeks in a sedate National Health Service nursing home, still shaking off its former life as a small hotel in Colwyn Bay on the Welsh coast. I can recall nothing of the place, apart from damp sea air and perpetual ominous migraines, born of a sense of sudden dislocation, and the smell of the tiny partitioned rooms - an amalgam of mould, inadequate drains, sawdust and fresh paint. I remember the quaint formality of our three daily meals, served in a dining room set with starched white linen table-cloths and gleaming pint-sized water glasses, provided, I can only assume, as a form of hydrotherapy.

Mother's condition at that time was overwhelmingly passive, speaking only when spoken to and, even then, reluctantly - apparently craving only to live within herself. She spent the afternoons in her bedroom, while I parcelled out long hours of time between *King Lear*, Hooke's Law and the austere opinions of W. B. Yeats on the poetry of his time. Each morning, we walked together along the windswept Promenade as far as a tennis club in its winter mode. Although not strictly a public place, the gates were invariably open and we installed ourselves on the deserted banks of concrete seating alongside the courts, sitting side by side, invalid blankets in startling red across our knees serving as tickets of admission. Mother watched with the same impassive intensity she committed to television cricket, contributing a little lonely applause at the conclusion of each exchange, to the evident discomfiture of the players.

As we walked back one day she took my arm, curling it inside her own, the way she would sometimes with Father on holidays. Of necessity, I usually led the way, but that day she turned abruptly into a side street, steering me briskly along. It was not our usual route and I hesitated, looking back in the direction of the tennis club, but she continued pulling, until I saw the familiar nursing home from its other side. Mother had spent part of her honeymoon in Colwyn Bay on her way to the rain-soaked Isle of Man, years before any of her boys existed. That faint remembrance of some seaside walk with Father was, I think, the first cruel sign of healing she would not live long enough to complete. I witnessed another that same day.

We were encouraged to gather in the lounge after an early dinner, where chess sets, playing cards and board games were set out, and generally left untouched. That evening, Mother noticed a pack of cards and asked *if I would like to play crib*. She had already opened the pack and motioned for me to sit opposite her at the table. She had been addicted to cribbage until illness put an end to such things. Watching her now, as she neatly shuffled the pack, demanding that I "cut", it seemed her hands had forgotten nothing. She dealt six cards each at impressive speed, setting the rest down at her side to turn the top card with a practised flip of one finger. I recalled enough of the rules to know I had to discard two cards, then count what my hand was worth, although exactly *how* defeated me. After long deliberation I remembered fifteen came into it and boldly claimed points for two cards that added up to that number. As she pegged my points on the board, I saw she was laughing quietly to herself, eyes bright in a face I realised I had not seen for years. She leaned forward, to take the cards from my hand, years falling away to reveal Mother as she had always been, teasingly impatient because she thought me slow. She spread my cards out, sorting them as she spoke: *look what you've got here, you silly girl: fifteen-two, fifteen four, and three for your run.* She triumphantly tapped a single card, the jack of clubs, almost giggling, *and one for his nob.*

We played for a good hour or more, Mother pegging victory in half a dozen games, the two of us hermetically encased in some tiny

174

bubble of space where everything was as it had always been. You would not know that this cheerful woman, effortlessly racking up yet one more complex score, smug with the craft of computation, only an hour before could not have told you where she was. No one would have known this was my mother, restored like Hermione to life, if only for a tiny scrap of time, gleefully calling, *fifteen-two, fifteen-four, four-for-a-run.*

*

I slept badly that night, tormented by thoughts beyond my understanding. Our game over, she had returned to her silent lifeless state. How had that tiny island of sanity come about? Where had it gone? How could some constellation of nerves possess the skill to play a childish game of cards, yet nothing else? Even that crass supposition collapsed the following day when I tried again with *cribbage.* She frowned at the word, staring wildly round the room, and said she wanted to go to bed. We never played again.

Chapter 22

I am in a narrow waiting room on the second floor of a building in Edmund Street, Birmingham. Through the single grimy window, I can just make out part of the pillared portico of the Town Hall. There are five of us, seated round something like a large dining table. Apart from Robert Alan Kennedy, 6S2, three girls in school uniform, although of a kind I do not recognise, and a very tall person, hardly a boy at all, wearing civilian clothes. In front of each, lies an ominous little booklet of lined paper. We have an hour in which to write something about music in Shakespeare's plays.

*

As to *why*, on that particular May morning, I found myself interviewed at length for a place to read English literature at Birmingham University, I can offer little by way of explanation, although a brief encounter towards the end of my first year in the sixth form must have played its part. I had been sought out in the prefects' room by that same Mr Eliot who had so cruelly dismissed my request to change courses. He admired my persistence, he said, and had been following my progress since I secured permission to alter course. Had I any intention of taking the study of literature further? I was lost for what to say. It had been Mother who secured that permission, not me. Mother, who perhaps had seen the pain of unrequited love and done what little she could to ease it - I will never know. All *inconsequential* now, in any case – illness had exacted its savage retribution on us both. I left Mr Eliot, half buried in books in his tiny room, unaware his innocent misconception had determined the course of my life.

I duly composed my essay on music in Shakespeare's plays, a complete ignorance of the subject licensing a number of highly implausible assertions about *The Winter's Tale* and *King Lear*, the only plays I was at all familiar with. Earlier timid exchanges with my fellow applicants, who seemed puzzled at how little I knew, had already convinced me I was engaged in a kind of make-believe. Whatever had piqued the interest of the mysterious interrogators who lay in wait that afternoon, it could not possibly have been my knowledge of English literature.

And so it proved. I was the final candidate called into the stuffy room, a coal fire still smoking in the grate. Three men were sprawled behind a table, patently fagged out by an afternoon of inquisition noisy enough for gusts of occasional laughter to have penetrated the door to where I had been seated, nervously waiting my turn. Assorted pages of my dismembered essay lay distributed among them. I had done the best I could with music in Hermione's restoration at the conclusion of *The Winter's Tale,* but the questions, when they arrived, were not at all concerned with that. Indeed, they were not about Shakespeare at all, still less about music. Asked to describe *life* in Ocker Hill - much as one might enquire of an Amazonian pygmy how he passed his days – I was pressed to say what games I played and what my hobbies were. I found myself overwhelmed with a sense of *déjà-vu.* It being almost summer, they did not mention skiing, but clearly these strange men had no appetite to hear what little I knew of Shakespeare - it was physics they had in mind. Artfully quizzed about the music of the spheres, I realised where I was being led. They might as well have asked about Uncle Leslie.

The leader, warming to his theme, said they had never interviewed a candidate with physics, chemistry and mathematics under his arm. Why would a scientist be interested in Shakespeare, he asked? Could I, as a *scientist* – now he had his teeth in the word, it seemed he could not let it go – could I, as a scientist, explain, in terms a layman would truly understand, *the physics of something*? He seemed aware the question was quite broad, but was already tamping tobacco in his pipe, fetching a spill from the fireplace to light it, smiling thoughtfully, much in the style of Jean Paul Satre. A complaisant, knowing, smile I had met before: not greatly different from that encountered after the Battle of the Gas Monitors. Suffused with a mixture of exasperation, triumph and shame, I felt myself ensnared. Whatever I did, their choice would fall on me. Not for the worth of anything I might say or know, it was a conclusion pre-ordained. The siren call of sociological experiment would drown out Shakespeare any day: I need hardly have been there at all. Albeit slightly under-nourished, this specimen of a caste they long had yearned to capture, was impossible to resist. I doubt the thought crossed a single mind that I might have had views on the matter.

I have no idea how long I spent describing the function of a triode valve: hours, it seemed, although it was probably less. My words, in any case, were largely Mr Bonar's, complete with tiny reflective pauses for questions, although none arose. It was a creditable performance, but the thought crossed my mind *in media res* that I was cheating my fellow postulants to the sacred order of letters, particularly a tall boy I never saw again, who had apparently dined on Elizabethan verse all his days. Explaining to a triptych of falsely attentive faces how the performance of a triode valve could be improved by the addition of a second grid, I could not but wonder what this had to do with Shakespeare; how knowing this peculiar fact could possibly unlock the sonnets of Sir Philip Sydney; ashamed to be engaged in a kind of intellectual fraud.

They got round to Shakespeare eventually. Given the request to recite a sonnet from memory, I managed, *Th' expense of spirit in a waste of shame* – a favourite of Joan's. It earned an arched exchange of knowing eyebrows between two of my interrogators and a weary: *D'you have anything less intense?* I stumbled through, *Shall I compare thee to a summer's day?* Asked to identify a play written entirely in verse, I received an approving nod for *Richard II*, but although I was sure I remembered enough of my speech to recite it, I was not asked. Given I claimed music was used to such powerful effect in *The Winter's Tale*, one asked, why did I think Shakespeare made use of it only in the last two acts? My mind completely blank, the frank confession I had no idea, produced only approving nods, somebody mumbling, *neither does anyone else, my boy.* And that was the end. I was dismissed on a genial tide of laughter and the assurance that English would take me - if, that is, *my A level was good enough.* They might, at least, have asked about *King Lear.*

*

It had hardly been a ruthless interrogation but left me feeling shabby, conscious I had somehow failed. Well aware my results could not possibly be good enough, they had had their sport. They no doubt thought it of little consequence, but the humiliation of the day, sealed with the empty promise *English would take me*, lived on. I had returned from distant Colwyn Bay to find a foreign school, my silent classmates revising things I had never seen. Expecting to be dismayed by the prospect of another year, I found myself embracing failure as a sweet relief. At least, I might avoid another afternoon prodded like a caged bear in Edmond Street.

I sat the examinations largely because my name had been enrolled. Freed from the constraint of preparation, my papers in English literature smacked of ill-concealed revenge. Someone must have read them, but what they made of my essay on *Lear and the Book of Job* is difficult to imagine. Written in fury, it combined reflections on some of the more morbid aspects of Methodism with a lament for lost goddesses. Lear, I argued with some passion, was not alone in losing all. Asked afterwards by Captain Maddox how I had got on, I said I thought I might have scraped a pass because I recognised one of the set poems as something of his own that Yeats considered modern verse. He agreed I would probably get credit for that, tactlessly adding that we would be doing *Hamlet* next year - a play he thought I would find greatly to my taste.

The long months of rhabdomyolysis had changed my little world. While I had been away, the silent hero of the school finally had died. Captain Aggleton returned from the First Great War incapable of teaching, to eke out his long remaining fearful years as a kind of school mascot. He spoke to me only once, flinging open the window of his upper-storey little cell to shout: *You, Kennedy down there, Uncle Joe's dead. Tell 'em that.* He had lived to say those words, they said. Although The Pot barely mentioned his death, and seemed to resent our devotion, the whole school attended Aggie's funeral. It was the end of something, although we did not quite know what.

His replacement was appointed to teach history, but his true passion was the theatre. In a few short weeks of reforming zeal, this impresario I had yet to meet, was to drag the school into the modern world. Above all, Brown gloated one happy day, play reading was at an end. No more reverent pilgrimages of the elect to hear The Pot read Shaw, an end to all that. Even Frenchie agreed it had outlived its time. I wondered how he came to know her secret name and thought his satisfaction might have been less had he ever actually attended a play reading, but remembering Joan handing back her yellow booklet, I knew I no longer cared. I was only ever there for Joan.

The Christmas Concert, too, had gone. Along with the quickstep, vaudeville had served its time. Jokes that only a year ago had left us helpless with laughter seemed childish now. In place of the high-kicking children of Oberkirchen was to be the stylish sophistication of *The Teahouse of the August Moon*. Brown had secured the part of Sakini, he said; *why not try for Colonel Purdy?* Joan had told him she had time for Lotus Blossom, even with her Scholarship exams next year. The play would put an end to the pointless segregation of girls, we would all rehearse together – *what did I think of that?*

*

Mildred was not there at Morning Service the Sunday of my return, but waiting on the steps as I left to go home. She took my arm to walk together. She didn't have time for Chapel now, she said, A levels were more important. She had had an offer of a place at the College in Birmingham to train to be a teacher, but she needed to pass them all. Was I really going to be Colonel Purdy, she said, because Ant had told her I was - she would certainly come if I did. Seeing my puzzled face she added, *his name's Anthony - he doesn't like you calling him Brown.*

She had not been alone in missing the service that morning: the congregation was half its usual size. For the Evening Service it barely numbered a dozen and few seemed willing to sing. I was tempted to accompany them on the swell organ, but settled on my usual registration, drowning a few sad voices in a nobler sound. I sat with the Minister in the vestry afterwards. It was the television, he said. Once serials had started on Sunday evening, people stayed at home to watch. As to why that might affect the morning attendance as well, you would have to ask a psychologist: he thought shame came into it. Saying you prefer watching *Jane Eyre* to talking to God must surely make you ashamed. There must be more to do with your life than sitting crouched in front of a screen. He didn't have a television himself; somebody had said it was bad for your eyes. He seemed more angry than mortified. Things would have turned out better if only God had had more faith in Mr Attlee. He was going to start on *Romans* this very month with the idea of talking about things that happened fifty years ago. *When Paul wrote it, Jesus had only been dead for fifty years. You won't remember, Alan, but I do. Fifty years is not so long ago. No time at all.*

Strange, the first political thought of my whole life should arrive that morning, sitting with this defiant man, reconciling himself to defeat behind a battered Methodist desk, shuffling pages dense with inky thoughts, hoping a schoolboy might agree. How could I possibly agree? He was wrong: hopelessly, irredeemably, wrong. Fifty years ago, Mahler had been alive and walking about – the impossibility of that very thought was enough for me. The world of Dolly Clandon was only fifty years ago but might as well have been five hundred. That world, and the fool who invented it, had no place for the likes of me – I had lived already long enough to know that much. The only question worth asking now was whether *The Teahouse of the August Moon* would offer anything more.

*

I hardly needed to audition for Colonel Purdy, the impresario said, the role had been reserved for me. True, the script said the character was running to fat, but a skinny Colonel would do just as well for what he had in mind. He was already very much at home, this History Man, on the transformed stage of our Assembly Hall, its Bösendorfer relegated to some distant other place, pink chalk marks staining the sacred polished floor. Joan and Ant sat watching as I read the part, perched side by side on a huge wicker costume basket. Sakini and Lotus Blossom - too much a pair, I thought; although Joan had hugged me when I first arrived, her eyes bright with tears, whispering close in my ear, *did you get lost again?* They applauded at the end and said I would be perfect in the part. I needed only to master the American voice, but that was easily done. I was made for

Colonel Purdy.

And so it might have been, had The Pot not intervened, calling me to his astonished room that very day, to say I need not repeat my year. Someone - no doubt baffled by reflections on the Book of Job - had awarded me the necessary grade in English literature. I was to embark on a university career, enrolled for an honours degree. A letter from the local authority about my grant - addressed not to Father, but to me - was already on its way.

*

I got up early on my appointed university day, intending to creep away like Oliver Twist before the house was awake, with only an apple to console my walk to Wednesbury station and a new and hollow world without Joan. To my surprise, there were voices downstairs and the lights were on in the living room. The tablecloth was set, and a bowl of cornflakes already in my place with a little jug of orange juice at its side - Mother knew I would never have taken the milk. Father was eating his breakfast, the sleeves of his dressing gown rolled back out of the way. He was trying to stop the *Daily Express* drooping across the tea cosy, grinning to himself to excuse what was clearly a tiny theatrical lapse. Mother had heard me arrive, calling cheerfully from the kitchen that she was making me a boiled egg and to sit myself down, *because your father will give you a lift to the station.* Just this once, she added, *now there was only Ian to catch the bus.* It was an insanely early hour for breakfast, pitch dark outside and Ian still in bed, but Mother watched me play my part in their little tableau, complete with orange juice. It was almost as if I would not be coming back.

Father had not been so accommodating the day I showed him the letter about my grant to study English literature at the university. His pursed lips silently rehearsing words that never arrived, he plainly resented my casual willingness to waste advantages that that had never come his way. I remember dreading that he would ask me *why?* I would have been hard pressed to find an answer. He gave me the letter back, saying he had kept a place at home for Stuart and would do the same for me; and that my bedroom was there for as long as I wanted it. The thought that it might not have been there had never occurred to me and he must have read the expression in my face, softening his tone to say that I shouldn't expect my mother to wait on me hand and foot.

I spent the next six years at Birmingham University. In all that time, I cannot recall Father ever again mentioning the subjects I was studying and neither my progress nor my prospects. For reasons I have never really understood, I became white space on the family page.

*

My first university day bore an uncanny resemblance to my first day as a child of King Edward, albeit without the empty satchel. I arrived, a little late, to be greeted by a harassed woman endlessly turning a single sheet of paper in her hands in search of something plainly hard to find. My French results, she said – my French wasn't there. A momentary spasm of anxiety seized my heart, but realising she could not possibly know the horrid secret of my French, I assured her I had passed, modestly omitting *creditably*. *No, no, not O level*, she said, I needed A level French for my Anglo-Saxon, *so where was it?* The insouciant reply that perhaps I had best not do Anglo-Saxon, whatever that was, if it required A level French, was greeted with evident relief. Not - as I would discover soon enough - because my troubles were at an end. To the contrary, I had precipitated a crisis so severe she could happily abandon me to other, and more powerful, hands. Murmuring, *stay where you are*, although I had no intention of fleeing, she vanished into the maze of Dickensian corridors behind her.

I was not kept waiting long, my head filled with dispiriting linguistic speculation. French had been bad enough, I thought: if the price of admission to English was yet more of it, I could always think again. By the time she returned, the sense of revulsion attached to the words *Anglo-Saxon* was well-established. I was taken to see Professor Spencer, who declared he had just arrived himself and barely settled

183

in. Someone, somewhere, somehow, seemed to have made a mistake because it was impossible to graduate in English without Anglo-Saxon. We were both newcomers, he added, but those were the rules: needs must when the devil drives. I would have to be patient and come back the following day, which would give him time to find a solution. On the journey home, I pulled out the battered script that had rarely left my briefcase and contentedly rehearsed a heated exchange between Colonel Purdy and Lotus Blossom in the second act.

*

It was not *wholly* desirable Professor Spencer said the following day. Indeed, it was hardly desirable at all, but he had found a solution. The Advisors of Studies who had interviewed me (no doubt bewitched by physics) had mistakenly admitted me to a course I was not qualified to pursue. It was not my fault, of course, but an A level in a foreign language was necessary to study English, as was completion of a course in Anglo-Saxon. These were not his rules – indeed, he thought them stupid – but they could not be changed now. However, all was not lost. Why not drop Anglo-Saxon, he asked, and replace the hours it would otherwise consume with something else? That way, I could forge a combined honours degree with another subject. *What did I think of that?* Since he seemed exercised by the matter, and far more anxious than me, I nodded my assent. As to what subject to select, alas, there was little choice, since a language was demanded for an Arts degree. Would perhaps *psychology*, he asked himself, sensibly complement the study of literature? I had the science subjects needed for that, and the man in charge was willing to take me.

I had listened to all this in something of a daze, but was sufficiently cheered by the removal of Anglo-Saxon from my life to hear myself say I would be more than interested because I had recently read *The Psychopathology of Everyday Life*. Forced to admit I had read only a translation – German, he had excitedly declared, would do just as well as French – he lapsed into gloomy silence. Indeed, it was only as I made to leave, that I understood why he seemed so much less cheerful than me. There was still the question of the language, he said,

I still needed a language. He had spent a long time on this question and had stumbled on an intriguing solution. Whoever drafted the regulations to study Italian for an Arts degree had failed to include a requirement for any prior study of the language at all. It was clearly peculiar, and certainly not intended, but I could take first-year Italian, albeit completely innocent of any prior contact with either Italy or its language. He hurried on in case I raised what seemed an obvious objection. He had discussed *the situation* with the man in charge, who agreed that it might not be quite as daunting as it first appeared. The first year in Italian was largely devoted to politics and literature, plays by Pirandello and the like. All in Italian, of course, but a student of English might well enjoy them. As for the language itself, I could join the group taking the refresher course - not in any way more demanding than an A level in Italian. If I worked hard, I would soon catch up: *any bright boy could manage that.* Once I'd got that out of the way, he said, I would be able to settle to my English and my ... my .... In the silence that had ensued I realised he had forgotten the other half of his quadratic. I mumbled *psychology* to help him along.

I could have waited for a bus when the train reached Wednesbury, but decided to walk home, crossing the hump-back bridge over the canal at the foot of Leabrook Road. I had often walked with Mildred under this bridge on Sundays, winding our devious route to the fields. It seemed unlikely we would have much time for all that now. Mother was in the kitchen when I got back. I told her I was going to do English, psychology and Italian at the university and the only compulsory PE course still free had been Fencing, but I didn't mind trying that. I think she said it seemed a lot.

*

My first tormented university year I'm sure was meant to end another way; but, in fact, I did not expire like Baron Corvo, in some doomed Italian lagoon. I squeaked an Italian pass and lived to spend another life searching to discover how words work. All that a passion born of a thoughtless compromise taken on a busy working day, many years ago. Possibly there is no secret walkway between words and things;

certainly, I never found it; but that does not mean that looking has been a waste of time. It is hard not to resent Professor Spencer's accidental Italian that so blighted a year of my university life, but I can, at least, turn it to psychic profit, confirming how little we retain of things so rapidly acquired. Hermann Ebbinghaus knew this long before Freud had any views at all on the workings of the human mind.

There is a scene towards the end of Pirandello's play *Henry IV*. Admitting he knew quite well he was no medieval king and that his madness was mere pretence, Enrico Quarto scorns his sycophantic aides: "This is my life! Quite a different thing from your life! Your life, the life in which you have grown old, I have not lived that life."

The author, Stourbridge, 1950

About the author

Alan Kennedy is emeritus professor of psychology at the University of Dundee, and was formerly a research associate at the Laboratoire de Psychologie et Neurosciences Cognitives, Paris Descartes University, Boulogne-Billancourt, France. A cognitive psychologist with a background in English Literature and Psychology, he played a significant role in establishing the new science of psycholinguistics in the UK and France. He is the author of numerous books and articles on the psychology of reading.

His writing career began with a series of childrens' books, including the best-selling "Ransomesque romance", *The Boat in the Bay*. His fiction for adults includes a World War Two spy trilogy, described by one critic as "a kind of literary fugue." Much of his fiction is set in France.

Kennedy has published a biography of the children's author Arthur Ransome (*A Thoroughly Mischievous Person: The Other Arthur Ransome*) and frequently writes and lectures on Ransome's use of myth and symbolism in his fiction.

He is Fellow of The Royal Society of Edinburgh, a member of the Society of Authors and an Honorary Member of The Experimental Psychology Society.

He lives near Marciac in the South-West of France.

By the same author

Fiction

The Boat in the Bay
The Broken Bell
The Pink House
Lucy
A Time to Tell Lies
The Things that are Lost
The War and Alex Vere (compilation)

Non-Fiction

The Psychology of Reading
Oscar & Lucy
A Most Mischievous Person - The Other Arther Ransome

www.ingramcontent.com/pod-product-compliance
Lightning Source LLC
Chambersburg PA
CBHW020855090426
42736CB00008B/388